IN THE YEAR OF MUNICH

IN THE YEAR OF MUNICH

Roy Douglas
Senior Lecturer, General Studies
University of Surrey

First published 1977 by
THE MACMILLAN PRESS LTD
*London and Basingstoke
Associated companies in Delhi
Dublin Hong Kong Johannesburg Lagos
Melbourne New York Singapore Tokyo*

British Library Cataloguing in Publication Data

Douglas, Roy, b.1924
    In the year of Munich.
    1. Munich four-power agreement, 1938   2. Europe
    – Politics and government – 1918 – 1945   3. Europe –
    History – 1918 – 1945
    I. Title
    940.53 12   D727

ISBN 0–333–22559–7

Printed in Great Britain by
BILLING AND SONS LTD
Guildford, Worcester and London

Contents

List of Plates

Acknowledgements

The author wishes to acknowledge many acts of kindness, without which this work would have been impossible. First he would like to thank his wife and Professor Otto Pick of the University of Surrey, who have read and criticised the manuscript. The faults which undoubtedly remain are those of the writer.

The author wishes to express his thanks to Librarians of the following institutions, who have kindly allowed him access to archive material: the Public Record Office; the House of Lords Record Office; the Bodleian Library; the University of Cambridge; the University of Birmingham; the University of Newcastle upon Tyne; Churchill College, Cambridge; University College, Oxford; the British Library of Political and Economic Science (London School of Economics); the Beaverbrook Library (whose archives are now at the House of Lords Record Office); the Labour Party. He also wishes to thank the following institutions and individuals for permission to quote material in which they have copyright: the University of Birmingham (Neville Chamberlain papers); the Public Record Office (Cabinet and Foreign Office papers); Her Majesty's Stationery Office (Documents on British Foreign Policy, 3rd series); the Marquess of Salisbury (Viscount Cranborne documents); Mary Duchess of Roxburghe (Marquess of Crewe documents); the British Library of Political and Economic Science (Lord Dalton diaries); The National Maritime Museum (Lord Chatfield papers); the Beaverbrook Library (Earl Lloyd-George papers); the Lady Avon (Earl of Avon documents); the Viscount Caldecote (1st Viscount Caldecote documents); the Earl of Halifax (1st Earl of Halifax documents); the Viscount Thurso (1st Viscount Thurso papers); the Hon. Godfrey Samuel, C.B.E. (Viscount Samuel papers); the Lady Vansittart (Lord Vansittart documents); the University of Newcastle upon Tyne (Viscount Runciman papers); the Viscount and Sir Steven Runciman (other Viscount Runciman copyrights); the Labour Party (Labour Party Executive Committee Minutes). The author fears that he may have omitted to obtain permission to quote some copyright material; if so, he offers his sincere apologies to the owners of any copyrights accidentally infringed. He trusts that they will appreciate that in some cases it is not immediately apparent in whom copyright ownership resides, and that literary heirs are very difficult to trace.

Finally, the author would like to acknowledge grants for expenses in connection with this work from the Faculty IV Research Fund of the University of Surrey.

One further point. A number of geographical and personal names were not, and are not, always spelt the same way. In those cases – even in quotations – the modern spelling has been followed.

January 1977　　　　　　　　　　　　　　　　　　　　Roy Douglas
University of Surrey
Guildford

1 Prelude

'I have been reading' "The House that Hitler built" – an exceedingly clever and well-informed but very pessimistic book. If I accepted the author's conclusions I should despair, but I don't and won't.'
Neville to Hilda Chamberlain, 30 January 1938. NC 18/1/1037

During the Second World War, an explanation of the origin of the war gained wide currency. That particular explanation is still largely believed.

According to this view, the 'National' Government which ruled Britain during most of the 1930s was to a very large extent culpable, both for failing to recognise and resist the menace from Germany, Italy and Japan at a time when they could have been resisted without war and also for grossly mishandling the first part of the war itself. During the crucial period, the National Government was constantly receiving advice and warning from much wiser people in the Labour and Liberal Parties, and also from a substantial section of the Conservative Party itself; but the Government ignored those warnings until it was too late to avert war, and almost too late to avert defeat.

In the past few years, a large number of documents have become available for study which throw much light on the information available to men of the time, and their motives in taking the decisions they did. The author decided to examine a part of the pre-war period in detail in order to test the various views. He has selected what will be called 'the Year of Munich'. For most purposes this begins in February 1938, when Germany began to exert pressure on Austria, and ends in March 1939, a few days after Germany had established her 'Protectorate' over Bohemia and Moravia.

During the Year of Munich, British opinion at all levels underwent an enormous change. At the beginning, most people seem to have believed that peace would – or at least could – be preserved for many years to come. At the end, it was generally considered unlikely that war could be averted, save at the price of complete surrender to the will of Adolf Hitler.

In this study the author will confine himself to information which we know, or have good reason for thinking, was available in Britain. Facts which were only known to people in foreign countries must be excluded, because it was impossible for people in Britain to act on those facts.It will be necessary to study the ideas and activities of people abroad – but from the angle of how they affected attitudes in Britain. The problem here is not what foreigners really did, or sought to do, but rather what British people considered they had done, or sought to do. So far as possible, the author will try to tell his story from documents of the period rather than the innumerable later interpretations.

It is important to remember that different people had access to different information. The man in the street, and even Opposition politicians, can scarcely be blamed for not having given proper weight to the gloomy and highly confidential document which the Chiefs of Staff circulated to the Cabinet in March 1938. On the other hand, a good deal of information about the extent and disposition of the world's armed forces was generally available.

It is useful to start from something rather like the 'presumption of innocence' in English criminal law: to presume that no one person or group of people in Britain possessed more or less of any moral or intellectual quality than others did – unless and until evidence arrives to the contrary. There is always a danger of assuming that people who were 'proved right' – whatever that means – by subsequent events were acting more wisely than those who were 'proved wrong'. That is by no means necessarily the case. It appears likely that some of the people who preached resistance to Germany in 1938 (and were thereby 'proved right' later on) would not have taken the stand they did if they had known and understood the military and diplomatic situation at the time.

When the treaties of peace were devised at the end of the First World War, the 'Big Four' Allied Powers who dominated the arrangements were the United States, Britain, France and (by courtesy) Italy. Germany was treated throughout as a defeated enemy. Austro-Hungary had already exploded into fragments just before the end of the war. The Russian Empire was still in the middle of civil war, and it was impossible to predict what states, still less what political systems, would survive the maelstrom.

In attempting to define the political frontiers of Europe, the Big Four were guided by certain general principles. The units they were creating must be, so far as possible, nationally cohesive, economically viable and militarily defensible; and historical frontiers should be respected. A fifth consideration, though stated less clearly, was also implied: that the defeated enemy should in no circumstances be placed in a better position than he had been before the war. These considerations were often in conflict. This applied, for example, in relation to Czechoslovakia. It was of great symbolic importance to the Czechs that the western boundary of the new state should correspond with the limits of historic Bohemia. This boundary was also a good one from the aspects of economics and military defence. Unfortunately this necessitated including within Czechoslovakia a large number of people whose language and culture were German, whose forebears had migrated into Bohemia during preceding centuries. Even more difficult problems affected Poland. The boundaries of historic

Poland had been far more fluid than the western limits of Bohemia. Most people of Polish speech and culture lived well inland; but if Poland was to be constituted as an independent state it required access to the sea. This could only be provided by cutting the Polish Corridor through an area of mixed population, sundering East Prussia from the main body of Germany and constituting the undeniably German town of Danzig a 'free city' under control of the League of Nations. Austria also posed exceedingly difficult problems for the peacemakers. When the Hungarian and Slavonic parts of the Habsburg Empire had departed, there remained a German-speaking rump. There were various possible solutions; but it was unthinkable that it should be attached to Germany.

Between 15° East and 30° East – roughly, the longitudes of Prague and Constantinople, from the Arctic Sea down to the Mediterranean – there existed a great wedge of petty states. The boundaries of all had been altered beyond recognition within living memory; most of them had only come into existence within the preceding twenty years. Nearly all of them contained large minorities – in some cases majorities – who were profoundly dissatisfied with existing territorial arrangements and hoped to see a drastic revision of those arrangements. Those who raised no complaint themselves had good reason to fear complaints from their neighbours.

On one side of that great wedge of land lay Germany; on the other Russia. Both had been shattered before the peace treaties were made; both would assuredly rise again, and make claims for economic or political infiltration in the area which lay between them. Who was in a position to resolve their conflicting claims – or to exclude them both – from an area which sooner or later they would both covet? Within the wedge itself, the only possible candidate was Poland; but it would take many, many years before Poland could be strong enough for such an enormous task. What of the countries which lay outside the wedge? The United States withdrew consciously and deliberately from all involvement in the affairs of Europe. The only possible guarantors of the settlement were therefore Britain, France and Italy. 'We all agree,' wrote Lord Chatfield, Chairman of the British Chiefs of Staff, at the beginning of 1937, '. . . we want peace; not only because we are a satisfied and therefore a peaceful people, but because it is in our imperial interests, having an exceedingly vulnerable empire, not to go to war . . .'[1] The same was true of France to an even greater extent. After 1918, Britain had acquired from Germany certain colonial mandated territories which were almost white elephants. France had acquired not only German overseas territories but also Alsace and Lorraine, provinces which had been an international football since the time of Louis XIV. Any major disturbance of the peace of Europe was likely to lead to the invasion of metropolitan France.

As they had been victors in a great war, and had acquired all that they could in any imaginable circumstances have desired, the whole strategic thinking of both Britain and France was defensive. In the 1930s the eastern border of France was protected by the Maginot Line – a great system of fortifications, designed to defend her from a German attack. In the Mediterranean, France maintained a substantial navy to protect her lines of communication. These tasks, though exacting, were not necessarily impossible to fulfil; but France had taken on other responsibilities which were far more difficult to discharge. In 1925, and against British advice, France had concluded treaties of mutual defence with Poland and Czechoslovakia, in order that her interest of containing German expansion westwards should be linked with their interest of containing expansion to the east.

The British navy was still the largest in the world, with the United States running rather a close second, and Japan third. The army was tiny and there was no military conscription. The Royal Air Force, unlike the French Air Force, was by no means insignificant in 1937 or early 1938; but the two Western Democracies combined had been outstripped by Germany in the air.

The question was often asked: Why need Britain bother herself with the affairs of continental Europe, and particularly the affairs of Central and Eastern Europe? Her concern with anything that struck at lines of communication with the Empire was undeniable. Britain, unlike any other major nation, depended on external sources for more than half of her food, and a very large proportion of her raw materials. Yet Central and Eastern Europe seemed of little importance to her from that point of view. Lord Chatfield explained the concern of a rather narrow imperialist for the fate of Central and Eastern Europe. Starting from the proposition that Britain's one 'vital interest' in Europe was in France and the Low Countries, Chatfield went on to argue:

> If Germany, realising this, as she could be made to realise it, tries to expand to the south east we must, in my opinion, accept it . . . If we are convinced that by German successes in Czechoslovakia, Poland, Romania and Danzig, she would eventually dominate Europe, and so threaten us at our front door or in the Near East, it would conceivably be better to fight her to prevent such domination, for the one thing that is quite clear to me is that Germany cannot remain as she is in the world.

These words were written a full year before Hitler's Germany transgressed any frontiers, and already express the dilemma which would face Britain if Germany turned Eastwards; while if Germany should turn to the west, Britain's existing treaty obligations to France and Belgium, as well as her vital interests, would be immediately engaged. It is not necessary to follow all of Lord Chatfield's arguments to accept the conclusion that Britain's continued power, and perhaps her very survival, depended on reducing the number of her potential enemies, or increasing the number of her potential allies; she would also need very rapidly to augment her defences. None of these processes could be brought about without cost.

In the 1930s the international order began to crumble. First challengers were the dissatisfied ex-Allies, Japan and Italy. In 1932 came the seizure of Manchukuo; then, in 1935, Italy attacked Abyssinia. Economic sanctions which Britain and France organised against Italy through the vehicle of the League of Nations proved ineffectual, and were soon abandoned. Thus did the Western Democracies secure the worst of both worlds; they had advertised their hostility by attempting to restrain or punish the agressor; they had proved their ineptitude by failing in the attempt.

In 1936 General Franco launched his attack on the 'Popular Front' Government of Spain: a broad coalition of the political left and centre. The Spanish Civil War continued, with immense slaughter and atrocities on both sides, until the early months of 1939. At first it was seen in Britain and France largely in ideological terms: the left, and a part of the right, supported the Spanish Government; a part of the right sympathised with Franco. As time went on, French views became nearly unanimous. In September 1937 Foreign Secretary Anthony Eden told the British Cabinet what he 'understood to be the view of the French General Staff, that the Italians sought submarine bases in Spain . . . The Spanish question had ceased to be one of politics of the left or of the right in France but had become one on which the General Staff view predominated.'[2] The British Government view as expressed to the Cabinet by the Prime Minister shortly afterwards was influenced by similar considerations: 'It did not matter o us which side won so long as it was a Spanish and not a German or an Italian victory.'[3] 'Activists' on the left in British politics remained preoccupied with the Spanish Civil War long after even greater dangers had appeared on the international scene. Sir Walter Citrine, one of the most important figures in the British Trade Union movement, commented to another leading Labour man in April 1938, 'Our own people were passionately concerned about Spain, but the great mass of the public were not.'[4] Sir Archibald Sinclair, leader of the Liberal Party, considered that the interests of Britain and France were 'more directly and vitally threatened' in Spain – where Italy was the principal external Power engaged – 'even than in Central Europe', where the threat undeniably came from Germany.[5] Labour Party Executive Committee minutes contain far more about Spain than about Central Europe until well past the middle of 1938.

The persistence of this attitude among British Opposition critics was perhaps not too serious; but greater perils were encountered when it remained a diplomatic obsession in France. In September 1937, Alexis Léger, Civil Service head of the French Foreign Office and a man of immense influence, argued that Hitler felt time to be on his side; that 'his share of the swag . . . will come to him without the use of force'; while Mussolini 'in order to obtain his share, requires a general conflagration.'[6] Nor was that preoccupation peculiar to France. On 2 February 1938, Eden told his Cabinet colleagues of a discussion which he had just had with eight other Foreign Ministers at the headquarters of the League of Nations. The main concern was over Italy; almost casually, the Cabinet minutes noted, 'He found that there was much less immediate anxiety about possible action by Germany.'[7]

Eden's own view was not dissimilar, though perhaps based on considerations of a more personal character. At the beginning of 1938 he wrote: '. . . There seems to be a certain difference between Italian German positions in that an agreement with the latter might have a chance of a reasonable life, especially if Hitler's own position were engaged, whereas Mussolini is, I feel, the complete gangster and his pledged word means nothing.'[8] What admitted of little doubt in the late 1930s was that the situation in Europe could change very dramatically, and perhaps very suddenly. These changes would present a serious danger of war, whose limits no man could foretell.

In May 1937 Prime Minister Stanley Baldwin resigned, and was succeeded by Neville Chamberlain, half-brother of the famous Sir Austen Chamberlain, and son of the even more famous Joseph. Baldwin had not kept a very firm hand on foreign policy; but, in so far as a foreign policy could be said to exist, that policy might be called 'Appeasement'. Anthony Eden, the young Foreign Secretary whom Chamberlain inherited from Baldwin, wrote at a much later date what 'Appeasement' had meant in 1936:

> I had by this time occasionally used the word 'Appeasement' in a speech or minute for the Foreign Office in the sense of the first meaning given in the *Oxford English Dictionary*, 'to bring peace, settle (strife, etc.)'. It was not until some years later, when the results of the foreign policy pursued by Mr. Chamberlain became apparent, that the word was more strongly associated with the last meaning given in the dictionary, 'to pacify, by satisfying demands'.[9]

This verbal ambiguity would lead to enormous misunderstanding.

From almost any view, there was much to be said for British statesmen making an effort to secure an understanding with Germany and Italy. Several months later Sir Maurice Hankey, Secretary to the Cabinet, who knew as much about Ministerial thinking as any human being, wrote a frank account of the situation as it stood in the late spring of 1937:

> When the present Prime Minister came into office he was determined to try and improve relations with Italy, and if possible with Germany . . . His motive was that he felt there was a drift going on towards war. Not only were we ourselves unprepared for war, but France, so far as we could judge, was equally unprepared, at any rate in the air and on the essential supply side. Moreover, ever since the breach with Italy over Abyssinia the Service authorities have been hammering in that it is impossible to conduct a war in the Far East, the West, and in the

Mediterranean on the line of communication between the two.[10]

Immediate apprehensions about the Far East were to some extent allayed in the course of 1937, as Japan became increasingly involved in war with China, which at least kept her hands from other mischief. Italy and Germany, however, had set up the so-called 'Rome–Berlin Axis', and were moving closer together; though, for most of 1937, the Axis was still less than an entente, let alone an alliance.

By contrast with the Foreign Secretary, the left and the French, most British officials came in the course of 1937 to perceive Germany as the more dangerous Axis Power. In July the Cabinet concurred with the view of the Committee of Imperial Defence that 'priority in defence preparations in Europe should be given to the provision of a deterrent to aggression by Germany.'[11] This made it particularly necessary to improve relations with Italy; which, in Chamberlain's view, would ensure 'that in the event of a dispute between ourselves and Germany the attitude of Italy would be very different from what it would be at present'.[12]

The greatest point of dispute between Britain and Italy concerned the latter's position in Abyssinia. Italians seem never to have believed that Britain's concern there was altruistic; they were convinced that it was motivated by fears for her colonial possessions in East Africa. The current situation was somewhat fatuous. Sanctions had long since disappeared; but the Italian conquest was not recognised by Britain or by the other League of Nations states. Nobody proposed to drive Italy from Abyssinia either by force or by economic means; but the consequence of non-recognition was that she had difficulty in raising international loans and displayed her ill-feeling by stirring up difficulties for the British authorities, particularly in Palestine and Egypt. More serious, this estrangement was clearly one of the most important considerations which were driving her towards association with the other 'isolated' Power, Germany.

On 27 July 1937, Chamberlain sent a personal letter to Mussolini, indicating that the British Government 'will be ready at any time to enter upon conversations with a view to clarifying the whole situation and removing all causes of suspicion or misunderstanding.'[13] One recurring feature of the period was that confidential information leaked freely into the French or Francophile press. This particular piece of news was published in the London *News Chronicle* before it reached the Duce. Mussolini, however, was not deterred, and eagerly accepted the suggestion. The British Ambassador in Rome, Sir Eric Drummond, was instructed to inform the Italians that 'we hope to see discussions started towards the end of August or beginning of September'.[14] Officials at the British Foreign Office seem to have had no doubt that this was a realistic date,[15] and it was certain that the Italians were eager. The proposed date was crucially important, for the League of Nations was due to meet at Geneva on 13 September. If general recognition of Italy's position was to be given, then the first step would be a declaration by the League that Abyssinia had ceased to exist as an independent state. A British initiative on the matter was likely to be followed.

As early as 19 August, however, there were signs that the Foreign Office preferred that talks should be delayed until after the League meeting.[16] On 26 August Franco's troops occupied Santander, and much publicity was given to the measure of support they had received from Italy. The French reacted sharply, and the original idea of talks before the League meeting gradually slipped out of sight. Eden, who had felt at the end of July that 'such a declaration might be made with general if not universal assent', now decided that 'any proposal of the kind . . . would meet with strong opposition.'[17]

If Britain would enter the talks which Mussolini desired, and make the recommendation which he sought, the League might still be useful to the Duce; if not, then he might surely be excused for thinking that it was a committee of his implacable enemies. On 25 September Mussolini visited Hitler at Munich.

The one great point of agreement between Britain, France and Italy had long been to preserve the separate identity of Austria, which ranked as an Italian 'satellite'. In 1934, when Chancellor Dollfuss was assassinated, Italy moved troops to the Brenner Pass to forestall a Nazi takeover. In the following year, not long before the attack on Abyssinia, the three countries had made a common declaration at Stresa in support of the preservation of Austria. There was no doubt that the Germans desired an 'Anschluss' – that is, a union – with Austria. This would be highly un-welcome to Italy, for it would open the door to German expansion in the Balkans and towards the Mediterranean. The Western Democracies had equally pressing reasons to exclude the Germans from Austria.

Just a few weeks too late, Sir Robert Vansittart, Permanent Under-Secretary for Foreign Affairs, perceived the baleful significance of the discussions between Hitler and Mussolini:

> The position of Austria has been causing us renewed anxiety lately. Not only may we suppose that this question was the subject of discussion between Mussolini and Hitler . . . but we have received reports from various sources which seem to show that we may have to reckon with the possibility of an *early* move by Germany designed to facilitate the absorption of Austria.[18]

The opportunity of an early *rapprochement* with Italy had been lost. Could the situation still be retrieved to some extent? A flurry of notes by senior Foreign Office officials confirmed their growing concern to come to terms with Italy as the sole means of checking Germany. 'There is no doubt whatever in my mind', wrote one man, 'that the delay . . . only serves to cement the Rome – Berlin Axis.' 'I agree,' added Sir Orme Sargent, the Assistant Under-Secretary,

I think that everything points to the fact that Mussolini, under great pressure, and much against his will, is being gradually forced by his German ally to withdraw entirely from Central Europe. The only thing which would really decide Mussolini to agree to this abdication would, I submit, be the conviction that he has from now onwards to face two hostile Powers in the Mediterranean and must therefore reduce his commitments in Central Europe so as to be able to concentrate his strength in the South . . .

Vansittart concurred laconically: 'I agree with these minutes. We are running unnecessary risks.'[19]

Their political chiefs, however, took a very different view. Viscount Cranborne, the Under-Secretary, gave the lead. He was preoccupied with the consequences of Abyssinian recognition: 'It would be a political blunder of the first water . . . It would profoundly shock large elements of opinion in this country . . .' Eden declared himself 'in entire agreement'.[20] One may, perhaps, enquire why these views had not been expressed with similar force several months earlier. There had been incidents in the Spanish Civil War which irritated and disturbed British and French opinion; but it would be difficult to argue that these incidents were of sufficient importance to require a radical shift of policy on such an important matter. There was much to be said for making no approach in the first place; there was much to be said for clinching an agreement. There was nothing to be said for vacillating from one view to the other.

Meanwhile, relations with Italy continued to deteriorate. The Italians seem to have entertained the suspicion – erroneous, but not unreasonable – that Britain was deliberately procrastinating until her rearmament had reached a point where she stood at clear advantage. Shortly before Christmas, the Earl of Perth (as Sir Eric Drummond had now become) wrote plaintively: 'We have today reached a vicious circle. Mussolini believes that we do not want to talk with him, and therefore does his best to make himself unpleasant in every possible way. We say that as long as he makes himself unpleasant we will not talk, and we both go round and round . . .'[21]

Such was the depressing picture of Anglo-Italian relations at the close of 1937. With Germany, however, the aspect seemed altogether brighter. In November Viscount Halifax, one of the most important members of the Government, was invited to Berlin – ostensibly in his capacity as a Master of the Hounds, to attend a hunting exhibition. In practice, the visit was conceived by both Governments as an occasion for informal political contacts – 'not to reach an agreement', as Chamberlain told the Cabinet, 'but to make contacts and to bring back to the Cabinet an impression of the German outlook and the possibilities of a settlement.'[22]

The general picture which Halifax brought back from Germany was encouraging. Amid some reservations about the reliability of a report

based on short encounters, he told his colleagues 'that the Germans had no
policy of immediate adventure. They were too busy building up their
country, which was still in a state of revolution. Nevertheless, he would
expect a beaver-like persistence in pursuing their aims in Central Europe,
but not in a form to give others cause – or probably occasion – to interfere.'
Lord Halifax concluded that 'the basis of an understanding might not be
too difficult as regards Central and Eastern Europe.' He was apparently
more worried about the question of the former German colonies, but even
here there seemed no cause for alarm. Göring 'had intimated that, even
with the colonial issue in the field, war was inconceivable.'

Vansittart, however, took a far less euphoric view. In what looks
uncommonly like a counterblast to Halifax, he circulated to the Cabinet a
depressing report, covered with the express request that his observations be
'treated as exceptionally secret:'

> For some months the radical section of the German National Socialist
> Party has been increasing its power and influence. This is particularly
> apparent in the additional supervision exercised by Himmler and the
> Gestapo . . . So far as the Government and Party can ensure it, the
> entire nation is being trained for war from the earliest age onwards; and
> the declared and open aim of the directors of German policy is to
> produce a machine so vast, so efficient, and so smooth-running that,
> once put into operation, it will move surely and automatically forward
> towards the accomplishment of World-Power. All my informants agree,
> not only that this is in fact the intention of Nazi policy, but that the Party
> has gone a very appreciable distance in the direction of carrying it out.[23]

On 1 January 1938 it was announced that Vansittart had been
transferred from his post as Permanent Under-Secretary of the Foreign
Office to a new and high-sounding appointment as Chief Diplomatic
Adviser to the Foreign Secretary; while the successor to his former office
was Sir Alexander Cadogan. The general drift of Vansittart's views on
Germany was well known, and the transfer was evidently a matter of
considerable importance. Diametrically opposite explanations were given:
ranging from the view that he would be 'to all intents and purposes another
Secretary of State' to the suggestion that he had been brushed aside – or
kicked upstairs. We are indebted to Sir Maurice Hankey for the real
reasons. The more or less official (though, of course, highly confidential) explanation was that most of the officials had been overladen
with immediate tasks; Vansittart would 'think out the numerous long-
range problems'.[24] Thus wrote Hankey to Sir Eric Phipps, Ambassador
in Paris; but on the same day he sent another letter to the same recipient,
which opens in an engaging manner: 'My typewritten letter is a discreet
one, which I can show to the P.M. This is not so discreet and more
informative.'[25] For more than a year, there had been 'a desire at the top for
a change at the F.O.' Vansittart 'refused to go abroad'. (The post actually

offered to him was Ambassador to France.[26] Hankey did not tell this to
Phipps, even in the 'indiscreet' letter.) There was 'an idea about that F.O.
suspiciousness has prevented us from taking advantage of the opportunities
to get on better terms with Italy and perhaps with Germany. The present
reorganisation is a way out of the difficulty.'

Vansittart assuredly had many enemies in high places. Early in
November he told Hugh Dalton, one of the main Labour spokesmen on
foreign affairs, that these included 'Londonderry, Lothian, *The Times*'. He
added that 'It was worse now because lots of people were frightened and
thought that by giving things away right and left to Germany they could
buy our own peace and security.'[27] Yet it is instructive to enquire why
Chamberlain and Eden, who were drifting further and further apart on
foreign policy questions, should have concurred in such an important step
as the transfer of Vansittart. Eden, who opposed the Italian approaches,
would naturally wish to remove the most important Foreign Office official
who supported them. Chamberlain was evidently influenced by
Vansittart's implacable hatred of Germany: 'when Anthony can work out
his ideas with a sane slow man like Alick Cadogan he will be much
steadier.'[28] He must have realised that Vansittart had originally opposed
the approach to Italy, but very likely did not yet appreciate that the
professionals at the Foreign Office had now swung round to his own
opinion on that question.

With Vansittart's transfer, Eden did not become more amenable to
Chamberlain's Italian policy, but rather less so. On the very day of the
announcement, the Foreign Secretary wrote about recognition of Italy's
position in Abyssinia, 'the more I look into it the more I dislike the idea of
this bargain'.[29] Between the Axis partners, there is little doubt where the
Foreign Secretary's preferences lay: 'As you know, I entirely agree that we
must make every effort to come to terms with Germany. The Italian
conversations are rather a different matter.'[30] Nor is there much doubt
from whom Eden received his anti-Italian opinions. A few days later he
communicated to Chamberlain another memorandum from Cranborne,
reaffirming his earlier views that the Italian talks 'would be an error, and
may be a disastrous error, of policy.'[31]

These letters had just been written when news came through of some
important Ministerial changes in Germany, which confirmed Vansittart's
assessment of the increasing importance of the more radical Nazis. Most
important of these was the replacement of Foreign Minister von Neurath
by von Ribbentrop, hitherto German Ambassador in London. The
advancement of von Ribbentrop was universally deplored in British
political and diplomatic circles; the one consolation was that any new
Ambassador would be an improvement. Thus wrote Chamberlain of von
Ribbentrop: 'He is so stupid, so shallow, so self-centred and self-satisfied so
totally devoid of intellectual capacity that he never seems to take in what is
said to him.'[32] The appointment signalled a marked change in German

foreign policy. From that point forth, Germany's interest in the recovery of her pre-1914 colonies – which had so troubled statesmen a few weeks before – became nominal and perfunctory. Her real concern was with expansion in Europe.

We may guess that one of the first people outside Germany itself to receive and evaluate the information was Benito Mussolini. Lady Chamberlain, widow of Sir Austen and a personal friend of the Duce, was then residing in Italy. Early in February she was requested to visit Mussolini. Lord Perth describes the upshot.

> She of course went. Signor Mussolini asked her whether she had recently had a letter from the Prime Minister and if so did she feel able to tell him its contents. Lady Chamberlain had received such a letter dated January 18 and she had told many of her friends and that the Prime Minister had stated in it that he expected to have Anglo-Italian conversations well started before the end of February.[33]

Lady Chamberlain reported the contents, which doubtless Mussolini already knew.

When Eden heard of this, he not unnaturally remonstrated with his chief. 'Without wishing to be unduly punctilious, I am sure you will understand that this kind of unorthodox diplomacy does place me in a most difficult position.' Chamberlain accepted the reproof, and promised to be more careful in future.[34] The real significance of this astonishing incident, however, is not so much the light which it throws upon the growing estrangement between Chamberlain and Eden, but rather what it suggests about Mussolini. He saw that action must be taken at once if Hitler were to be checked; and this action required the rapid conclusion of an understanding between Britain and Italy.

Within the next day or two, baleful news began to pour in from Austria. On 7 February the German Minister in Vienna proposed a meeting between Hitler and the Austrian Chancellor, von Schuschnigg, which eventually took place five days later. Von Schuschnigg was browbeaten, and forced to make two vital Nazi appointments in his government. His attempt to contact Mussolini, acknowledged 'protector' of Austrian independence, failed. Chamberlain viewed the new developments with considerable alarm, and told the Cabinet, 'Europe has received another lesson as to the methods by which Germany would pursue her aims. It was difficult to believe that this effort was the last, or that the eventual result would not be the absorption of Austria and probably some action in Czechoslovakia. That produced a dangerous situation . . .'[35] The Prime Minister went on to observe that 'this must be unpalatable to Signor Mussolini and that an opportunity offered to encourage him to make a more determined stand.' The opportunity envisaged was obviously the rapid inauguration of Anglo-Italian conversations. As Hankey noted privately, 'every pretext [had] been seized upon to delay conversations.'[36]

Chamberlain's dissatisfaction with the Foreign Office had clearly not been allayed as a result of Vansittart's transfer. Early in 1938, Eden had a brief rest in the South of France, and Chamberlain took temporary charge of his Department. Count Grandi, Italian Ambassador in London, was away in his own country at the time, but took the occasion as an opportunity not to be missed. There is a considerable element of farce in what followed. 'Grandi hastened back, presumably to see him while he was in charge. The Foreign Secretary returning from the South of France beat the Ambassador by a short head.'[37]

In Hankey's judgement, the Italian question was urgent for two reasons. In the first place, Hitler was to return Mussolini's visit in May, 'and after that the Rome–Berlin "axis" may become too tight for any agreement.' The second reason was a new aspect of an old problem.

> Our trump card has always been to recognise Italy's position in Abyssinia and lead the world in doing so. Quite a good part of the world has already recognised; every day we hear of someone going the same way: Holland yesterday, Belgium today, Turkey and the Balkan States tomorrow, and so forth. The trump card will soon have no value.[38]

Meanwhile, in Rome, Lord Perth was subjected to a considerable bombardment from people who urged that Britain should inaugurate the negotiations very soon. Count Ciano, Italian Foreign Secretary and son-in-law of Mussolini, was hardly a disinterested party; but he pressed, rather mysteriously, for 'an early start . . . in view of the possibility of certain future happenings'.[39] Others, whom no one could accuse of sympathy with the aspirations of Italian Fascism, expressed the same views even more forcefully:

> Both Soviet Ambassador and Czech Minister express the opinion this evening that the only thing which could prevent further German encroachment on Austrian independence would be early conclusion of a general agreement between Italy and ourselves. If this happens Signor Mussolini's hands would be much freer in order to combat German expansion in Central Europe. French chargé d'Affaires also considers that if Italians wish to ensure independence of Austria it is essential for them to come to terms with us.[40]

Lady Chamberlain was again used as a diplomatic intermediary, and on 17 February lunched with Ciano. She sent a message to her brother-in-law through the Ambassador in Rome. Ciano, she reported, 'begged me to let you know "time is everything. Today an agreement will be easy but things are happening in Europe which will make it impossible tomorrow." Lady Chamberlain found Count Ciano completely changed and states that he seemed intensely worried.'[41]

At long last, on Friday 18 February, Chamberlain, Eden and Grandi met. Italy, explained Grandi, had been expecting German encroachment on Austria, 'but it was not the result of an agreement . . . Now . . . there was nothing to be done owing to the state of relations between the Stresa Powers.'[42] Pressed about future there, Grandi

> said that possibly we were only at the end of the third act out of four. In the view of Italy, however, Germany was now at the Brenner. It was impossible for Italy to be left alone in the world with two great potential enemies – Germany and Great Britain . . . If it was impossible to improve relations with Great Britain then it would be necessary for Italy to draw still closer to Germany. The decision would then be final. It was not final yet, but there was very little time left.

Grandi was to return that afternoon. Eden refused to agree that he should be told that Britain was willing to enter formal conversations.[43]

Next day, Saturday 19 February, an emergency meeting of the Cabinet was called. Even Halifax, who was in much closer touch with the Prime Minister than most of his colleagues, had no inkling of the storm which was brewing.[44] After a long and apparently tedious introduction, Chamberlain led up to the proposal that talks with Italy should commence forthwith: a view with which most of his colleagues concurred. Eden thereupon threatened resignation. He told the Cabinet that he doubted Mussolini's change of heart, and thought that conversations should be delayed pending evidence that he had really undergone such a conversion. On the face of it, a mere dispute on a point of timing seemed a slight issue for the resignation of a young Minister who had already attained a very senior post in the Government. The Cabinet adjourned.[45]

After the meeting, Halifax and Oliver Stanley – President of the Board of Trade – went to the Foreign Office where they met Eden, Cranborne, and Eden's Foreign Office Secretary. From Halifax's account

> . . . I felt at once that the atmosphere, emanating, I thought, mainly from [Cranborne], was very much pro resignation . . . I could almost hear them saying, I thought, 'You have done very well. You have won the first round. Hold firm and all will be well.' . . . When we came away Oliver Stanley said to me, 'He's been through Hell to make up his mind, and he's d— well not going to un-make it.'[46]

The following day the Cabinet met again. Chamberlain explained that he had had a further talk with Eden. There was 'in addition to the difference of approach and method, a fundamental difference of opinion between them that he thought made further collaboration very difficult.' There was now a general explosion, initiated by Oliver Stanley: 'If there was a fundamental difference between the Prime Minister and the Foreign Secretary the Cabinet was entitled to know what it was, and that to be told of it in this way, and at such a time, was to place the Cabinet in a quite impossible position.'[47] Halifax attempted to damp things down, and proposed a small negotiating committee to attempt reconciliation. In the next few hours a series of meetings took place between various Ministers, and many possibilities were discussed – including the resignations of several members of the Cabinet, and even driving out Chamberlain himself. Later in the day, the Cabinet met again. By that time tempers had cooled and minds had clarified. Eden would resign; no other member of the Cabinet would go, though it was inevitable that Cranborne should follow his chief.

It was obviously impossible for either Chamberlain or Eden to make a full public statement of what the differences had been, either in the exchange of published letters or in the Parliamentary debate which supervened. Chamberlain could not say that he had been stalled for more than half a year, and at last forced the issue in the hope of averting an Italo-German alliance. Eden could not explain that the original approach to Mussolini had made been over his head, yet he made no move to resign; he went finally because he distrusted the honour of a foreign head of government. Nor could either statesman discuss at length the very different attitudes which they had taken to certain recent approaches by President Roosevelt of the United States. Eden evidently believed that immediate talks with Italy would vitiate a promising opportunity to involve America as a kind of *deus ex machina* in European affairs; Chamberlain, with equal conviction, seems to have thought that there was little chance of Roosevelt carrying his country very far towards any critical involvement.[48] In the circumstances, wildly different interpretations could be set on the dispute. 'Hawks' like Churchill and Lloyd George could see Eden as the apostle of resistance to both dictators. Lord Crewe, with the mind of a diplomat, guessed that he judged the moment tactically wrong for negotiations.[49] Most of the Liberals implied that he had been sacrificed for devotion to the League of Nations.[50] The Parliamentary debate which followed turned on a censure motion from the Labour Party, and the vote showed a perceptible revolt on the Government benches. One Conservative, Vyvyan Adams, voted with the Opposition. Seventeen others – including Eden, Cranborne, Churchill and Harold Macmillan – all abstained.

Eden was swiftly replaced at the Foreign Office by Lord Halifax, whom Chamberlain found a much more acceptable colleague – though not as pliant as later mythology has suggested. Eden, for a variety of reasons, rather played down the dispute, and later correspondence suggests that he was soon ready to consider a return to the Government.

Just as the view which sees Eden as the implacable opponent of any understanding with dictators is demonstrably wrong, so also is it wrong to think that those who opposed Eden in the Cabinet were necessarily 'appeasers' in the sense which that word eventually acquired. It will later be necessary to consider the resignation of Duff Cooper in the autumn of the same year on an even more dramatic issue of foreign policy; yet at the time of Eden's departure he was as strong a supporter of Chamberlain's view as any man in the Cabinet: and for the very reason that he perceived an agreement with Italy to be essential in order to counter the greater danger from Germany.

Like the question of German colonies, the Italian conversations would soon be by-passed by events. An Anglo-Italian agreement was in fact concluded on 16 April. It presaged recognition of the Abyssinian conquest, and was the cause of much bitter comment; but Italy had by then long ceased to be the most urgent matter for diplomatic concern. Yet perhaps the agreement performed some useful function. With the danger from Italy somewhat abated, Britain was more free to resist German pressure. For a good many months to come, Mussolini was far from being Hitler's obedient vassal. He was in no mood to pull Germany's chestnuts from the fire, and at one critical moment at least his intervention with Hitler may have proved of inestimable importance for the democratic states.

2 The Flood Gates Open

'Dr. Schuschnigg therefore is fighting a losing battle, and Austria will before long fall like a ripe plum into Hitler's maw, without any necessity for violence on the latter's part.'   Sir Eric Phipps to Anthony Eden, 10 October 1937, quoting views of Léon Blum. PHPP 1/19, fo. 18

Not the least remarkable feature of the controversy attending Eden's resignation was Neville Chamberlain's speech in the Parliamentary debate which followed. Answering Labour's censure motion, the Prime Minister went a good deal further than the occasion absolutely demanded:

> At the last election it was still possible to hope that the League might afford Collective Security. I believed it myself. I do not believe it now. I would say more. If I am right, as I am confident I am, in saying that the League as constituted today is unable to provide Collective Security for anybody, then I say that we must not try to delude ourselves, and still more we must not try to deceive small weak nations into thinking that they will be protected by the League against aggression and acting accordingly, when we know that nothing of the kind can be expected.

This statement was widely and bitterly quoted by the Government's critics in the months which followed. It seriously disturbed two junior Ministers, who wrote anxiously to Chamberlain, seeking an explanation.[1]

Yet the Government had still not taken full measure of the situation. Grandi's remark about Germany being at the Brenner was circulated to the Cabinet as part of the report of the interview, before their 'crisis' meeting of 19 February; but the minutes of that meeting do not suggest that its significance had been measured. Chamberlain himself suggested that the conversations with Italy which he desired would – if successful – 'give courage . . . to Austria.'[2] More than a week later, on 2 March, the Cabinet accepted the view that in the 'forthcoming negotiations with Germany . . . perhaps the most difficult question to be considered . . . was that of the colonies.'[3]

Although the fate of Austria had probably been decided, Chancellor Schuschnigg unwittingly hastened his country's doom. On 9 March he announced a plebiscite in Austria, at which he would seek support for the somewhat uncertain policy of his Government. The semi-official view was that all provinces except Styria would be likely to give a large majority to the Chancellor. Sir Nevile Henderson, Ambassador to Berlin, declared that Schuschnigg 'seems to have taken a leaf out of the Nazi book', and forecast 'much storm here'.[4]

On 11 March the Germans first demanded postponement of the plebiscite, then the dismissal of Schuschnigg and appointment of a government with a Nazi majority. At the last moment Schuschnigg contacted Halifax, who consulted Chamberlain, and then replied, in effect, that it was impossible for Britain to help.[5] Later the same day, German troops began to cross the Austrian frontier. On the following morning the Cabinet was convened. The minutes of that meeting describe the situation rather well: 'The Prime Minister said that although there was probably not very much that could be done, he had thought it right that the Cabinet should meet.'[6]

Britain sent a formal reproof through Sir Nevile Henderson. In the course of his interview with General Göring, Henderson made an unauthorised qualification which somewhat reduced the force of his *démarche*. This drew from Halifax a sharp and angry retort to the Ambassador.[7]

In the aftermath of the *Anschluss*, various theories were advanced as to the surrounding circumstances. Henderson had apparently believed for many years that Austria would eventually pass to the Reich; but he had also believed that she might assume a role of semi-independence, rather like pre-war Bavaria.[8] The Nazi story, communicated by Göring to a British journalist, was that there had been no intention immediately to absorb Austria into the Reich, even when German troops were pouring over the frontier; what suddenly changed the Führer's mind was the ecstatic reception he received in Linz, with the repeated shouts of 'Ein Volk! Ein Reich! Ein Führer?'[9]

From Austria's point of view, the difference between German tutelage and actual incorporation in the Reich may have been small; but the effect on future German policy was enormous. With Austria still nominally independent, at least the frontiers of Central Europe would have remained unchanged. The incorporation of Czechoslovak territory within the Reich could hardly be the first step on the German march to world power; but it could very easily be the second.

Many people sensed a possible link between Eden's resignation on 20 February and the invasion of Austria on 11 March. If such a link existed, there were two possible explanations. To the Government's critics, Eden had been 'sacrificed' because he wished to 'stand up to the dictators' and the Prime Minister did not. On that view, the *Anschluss* proved that Eden had been right and Chamberlain wrong. Another very different explanation was also possible: that Eden went because he had failed to see that Germany was incomparably the greater menace of the central dictatorships, and that the only chance of deterring Germany from a programme of aggression was by concluding some kind of deal with Italy.

On 13 March Chamberlain wrote reflectively to his sister: 'It is tragic to think that this might have been prevented if I had had Halifax at the F.O. instead of Anthony at the time I wrote my letter to Mussolini.'[10] Perhaps a great deal more damage could have been prevented too.

The *Anschluss* focused world attention on future German designs. Czechoslovakia was obviously menaced. Long before the crucial events in Austria, British Cabinet discussions had been full of references to Czechoslovakia. Particular concern was felt over the Sudetenland: the area fringing the western border, where the population was predominantly German in speech and culture.

Hitler made no secret of the fact that he sought some changes in relation to the Sudetenland, but it was by no means certain as yet what those changes were – or even whether the Führer had formulated them clearly in his own mind. At the time of the *Anschluss* Field Marshal Göring, one of the principal Nazi leaders, assured the Czech Minister in Berlin that 'the developments in Austria will in no way have any detrimental influence on the relations between the German Reich and Czechoslovakia.'[11] Göring's rhetorical flourish, 'Ich gebe Ihnen mein Ehrenwort' – 'I give you my word of honour', was regarded by Halifax with a measure of cynicism; but nobody could yet be certain that Göring lied. On the other hand, there was much reason for apprehension. Vansittart received report of a speech which the same Göring was said to have delivered to high German officials more than a month before the *Anschluss*, and Göring's *Ehrenwort* to the Czechs. He was alleged to have foreshadowed the annexation first of Austria and then of Czechoslovakia, which would take place

> before the slow-moving Western Democracies would have mobilised their forces into any line of intervention . . . Faced with a *fait accompli*, [they] would then not resort to arms but would deliberate and make verbal protests as ever. Thereafter Hungary and the Balkan States would automatically come under Germany's economic dictatorship.[12]

Vansittart's anti-German views were well known; but Sir Nevile Henderson showed the not unusual Ambassadorial propensity towards sympathy with the country to which he was accredited. Henderson's view of likely German designs was little, if any, more comforting than that of Vansittart himself. In a despatch sent at the beginning of April, Henderson argued that after Hitler had received satisfaction in the Sudetenland, 'a solution of the [Polish] Corridor, together with a possible rectification of the Silesian frontier, constitutes his third main objective. Danzig and Memel must be regarded as subordinate questions.'[13] While Henderson felt that 'Any material advance beyond those limits, except insofar as colonies are concerned, is . . . not only hypothetical but contrary to Hitler's own doctrine of nationality of a pure German race' – yet even he did not exclude eventual German moves in 'the Ukraine . . . Romania's oilfields [and] outlets on the Mediterranean via Trieste or the Balkans.'

Thus the British Government had good grounds for grave apprehensions about Germany's long-term aims, quite apart from the sombre words of Hitler's celebrated *Mein Kampf*. For the time being, however, it was no more than suspicion.

British soldiers and statesmen had long considered the possibility that at some future date they might be involved in war with Germany as allies of France. In the spring of 1936, German troops reoccupied the Rhineland, which had been demilitarised under the Peace Treaties. Germany was in no immediate position to attack anybody; but the move could be seen as a long-term threat to France. True, no doubt, Germany was walking into her own back garden; but why should she choose to do so, and in a manner which was certain to frighten the neighbours? The possibility of British involvement arose, and the Chiefs of Staff were instructed to compile an 'appreciation' of the situation which would arise in the event of war with Germany three years later. Their provisional report was produced, as a highly secret document, in October 1936;[14] although almost any amateur strategist could have guessed the general drift of the argument. The Chiefs of Staff assumed that such a war would result from a German attack on France, or Belgium, or both of them; that the belligerents would be Britain, France and Belgium on one side and Germany on the other. Italy would 'probably be sympathetic to Germany but we hope initially neutral'. The general conclusion was that the Allies would be superior at sea, while at first the Germans would be superior on land, and probably in the air. German strategy, the Chiefs of Staff considered, would turn on an early knock-out blow. If this could be withstood, the greater industrial and economic potential of the Allies would be called into play, and a destroying counter-attack could eventually be launched.

Thus in 1936 it had been generally assumed that any future war between the Western Democracies and Germany must necessarily arise from a German attack in the west. At the time, there had been much in favour of that point of view. Germany's significant eastern neighbours were Poland and Czechoslovakia. Not only was Poland considered by some to have a very powerful army, but for a variety of reasons – political as well as military – war between the two countries was generally thought to be extremely unlikely. As for the Czechs, they possessed impressive field defences on their frontier with the Reich, and a strong army as well. Therefore, the only German war for which Britain and France need prepare themselves was a defensive war against a German attack in the west. No doubt there were unfortunate and dangerous features in their situation: the Maginot Line did not extend to the sea, and France in particular had not woken up to the growing importance of the air; but nevertheless the strategists seem on the whole to have been satisfied, provided that proper attention could be given to a modest programme of rearmament. Britain's most glaring weakness was in her land forces. Whether or not there was a strong argument for greatly increasing these in order to render substantial help to France in time of need, there was no shadow of doubt that public opinion would have reacted with the greatest possible indignation to any suggestion that Britain should be saddled with a large and costly army – particularly if this also involved compulsory military service. The British Government had enough trouble as it was in persuading the nation to accept rearmament. Whatever else entered into the calculations, nobody seems to have given much attention to the idea that the role of the Western Democracies might be an offensive one, designed to relieve pressure on an eastern ally.

When Czechoslovakia became the next likely target for Hitler's designs, nearly all this thinking was swept aside. The impressive defences, both natural and artificial, along the Bohemian mountains had been largely by-passed; the frontier with former Austria was plainland, and practically unfortified. As has been noted, even Henderson accepted that German control over Czechoslovakia could swiftly lead to a German hegemony over south-east Europe, to say the very least. Such a hegemony would upset the whole balance of power in Europe, if not throughout the world, to the immense detriment of Britain and France. More immediately, the French treaty with Czechoslovakia would be activated if Germany invaded and the Czechs resisted.

Another Power was also brought into the calculations: the Soviet Union. She also had a treaty with Czechoslovakia, and of much more recent date. This, however, was not a simple mutual assistance treaty; for Russia only undertook to go to Czechoslovakia's defence if the French had already engaged themselves in war on behalf of the Czechs.

The Soviet Union excited the deepest and most conflicting passions in all countries and social groups; and the differences by no means followed closely the ordinary divisions of 'right' and 'left', however we define those elusive terms. Yet, broadly speaking, official British opinion − Government, diplomatic and military – seems to have viewed the Soviet Union from an essentially strategic angle. People were much more worried about whether Russia would be a significant asset in a war designed to contain Germany, than whether she was likely to inaugurate world revolution. Vast suspicion existed on both sides. Chamberlain wrote of 'the Russians stealthily and cunningly pulling all the strings behind the scenes to get us involved in war with Germany (our secret service doesn't spend all the time looking out of the window)'.[15] The emotional character of this observation is significant; for, boiled down, it means no more than that the Soviet Union, like every other country in the world, preferred to get other people to fight its battles if possible. At the time, however, nobody doubted that Russia eagerly desired the downfall of Hitler, and was far more likely to be an ally than an enemy in the event of war. How useful was Russia as a potential ally?

In 1937, the Red Army 'purges' had been at their height. In the opinion of the British Military Attaché in Moscow, no fewer than 65 per cent of the

higher ranks had been wiped out; while parallel purges had occurred
elsewhere in Soviet life. The disorganisation which had resulted in all
branches of production, distribution and transport would certainly prove
highly detrimental in time of war. Eventually, the Attaché considered,
Russia would 'play an extremely important role in world affairs' – but not
yet.[16] The British Labour Party's Advisory Committee on International
Relations had similar doubts 'about Russia's real strength and real loyalty
to the League's cause'.[17] They added a disconcerting rider: 'Without
Russia's power the League's sum won't come out'. We may wonder
whether the sum would come out, even with Russia's power. The Labour
Party, having raised the question, never really answered it – or rather, they
assumed that the answer would be a satisfactory one, and – like most
critics – proceeded thereafter to look at the matter from a diplomatic
rather than a military angle.

The most extraordinary feature of the Russian treaty with
Czechoslovakia was that in 1938 the Soviet Union had no common frontier
with either Czechoslovakia or Germany. How, then, could she deploy her
forces in support of Czechoslovakia, even if she possessed both the will and
the might to engage Germany in war, should need arise? The Soviet Union
belonged to the League of Nations – and the Covenant of the League
included an obligation by member-states to afford passage through their
territory to the forces of other countries acting in accordance with the
League's recommendations. If, therefore, war broke out between
Germany and Czechoslovakia, and the League pronounced Germany the
aggressor, then Russia could demand right of passage through intervening
countries which belonged to the League.

A day or two after the *Anschluss*, Litvinov, the Soviet Foreign Secretary,
gave a press conference. He reaffirmed the Russo-Czech Treaty, and the
Soviet intention to fulfil its terms. Viscount Chilston, Ambassador to
Moscow and son of a famous Conservative Chief Whip, recorded that
Litvinov 'certainly told them that USSR would intervene in defence of
Czechoslovakia if France did, and when pressed to state how this would be
accomplished in the absence of a common frontier, he appears to have
replied, "Means would be found."'[18] Chilston regarded this as bluff, not
believing that Russia would fight. But what if Litvinov was not bluffing,
and the Soviet Union really did propose to fulfil her treaty: what 'means'
could be 'found'? The British, French and Czech Military Attachés in
Moscow discussed the question. They agreed that the route would have to
be through Poland. Russia would demand passage. In the likely event of
Poland refusing, Russia would declare war on the Poles.[19]

Another disturbing feature of the situation was the character of the state,
Czechoslovakia, which might soon become the nominal cause of a great
European war. The total population was around $14\frac{1}{2}$ millions. The two
eponymous races were both Slavs, and spoke related languages; but their
histories and current conditions were very different. The Czechs, who

formed something like half of the total population of the country, were predominantly Protestant, and had constituted the nucleus of the Kingdom of Bohemia, which was incorporated in the Habsburg land early in the seventeenth century. The Slovaks, about 20 per cent of the total and predominantly Catholic, had belonged to Hungary. They had eventually been taken into the Habsburg Empire along with the Magyars themselves. When the Empire was divided into two autonomous units, the Czechs went with Austria, the Slovaks with Hungary. About 23 per cent of the country's population were Sudetendeutsch, about 4 per cent were Magyars, and there were smaller groups of Ruthenians, Poles and others.

Under the Habsburgs, the Czechs felt themselves victims of pro-German discrimination; under the Republic the Sudetendeutsch considered themselves victims of pro-Czech discrimination. This discrimination certainly did not amount to persecution, and it was often pointed out that the Sudetendeutsch were at least as well treated as any ethnic minority in Europe. On the other hand, there was little doubt that the Czechs did tend in many ways to behave as a 'master race'. They received a very disproportionate number of Government posts. When large German landowners had their land expropriated at the end of the war, the incoming peasants were mainly Czechs. Complaints were raised about Czech schools being built in non-Czech areas, about emphasis on the Czech language, and about Government orders being given preferentially to Czech firms and so on. In times of heavy unemployment the largely industrial Sudetendeutsch suffered more than the mainly agrarian Czechs, which added to the sense of grievance.[20] That implacable opponent of Nazism, Sir Robert Vansittart, considered that Czech police methods were 'not very civilised', and deplored the practice of Czech Ministers and politicians who had treated the Sudeten leader Henlein as 'a social and political outcast'.[21]

One might adduce other unfortunate features of the Czechoslovak state. In the eastern districts, illiteracy was exceedingly high. The government turned on a coalition of no fewer than five political parties – the 'velkà pĕtka. Basil Newton, British Minister in Prague and an astute observer, wrote that

> quick and clear decisions were hard to come by, and party considerations were only too often given pride of place over national. Moreover, it is hardly an exaggeration to say that all public appointments, even down to that of crossing-sweeper, depended upon possession of the necessary party ticket, so that each party became almost a State within the State.[22]

Yet, for all its imperfections, Czechoslovakia was the only country in Central or Eastern Europe which could possibly be called a democracy, and it therefore possessed a strong emotional appeal to those people in Britain and France who were alarmed at the spread of dictatorships of one form or another. For that reason, such people tended to reject as spurious those real grievances that the Sudetendeutsch possessed, and did not always exert as much pressure as they should have done to persuade the Czechoslovak Government to rectify them.

British diplomatic reports from Vienna show that the Austrians gave at least the superficial appearance of welcoming the *Anschluss*.[23] The Sudetendeutsch, who until less than twenty years earlier had been fellow-citizens of the Habsburg monarchy, were profoundly stirred. Within a week, the British consul in one Sudeten town reported that events in Austria had

> set in motion an avalanche of national feeling among the Sudeten Germans which will soon lead to a united front of all Germans in the State and will be hard to control unless the Government is prepared to make concessions. The excitement and enthusiasm of everybody is very great indeed, and the feeling is growing that the problem of the Sudeten Germans will have to be resolved in the near future.[24]

All of these matters led to a growing concern about how Britain should behave in this undeniably serious situation. On 15 March 1938 J. Paul-Boncour, French Foreign Secretary, had an interview with Sir Eric Phipps, in which he 'urged that His Majesty's Government should declare publicly that if Germany attacked Czechoslovakia and France went to the latter's assistance, Great Britain would stand by France.'[25] Chamberlain and Halifax were at first receptive of such proposals. The same day, Hankey reported that they were contemplating two possible courses of action: acceptance of the French proposal as it stood; or, alternatively, 'that we might form up in support of the French some sort of grand alliance, nominally, at least, under the aegis of the League of Nations, to guarantee Czechoslovakia against an alteration of her frontier by force.'[26] A document was promptly drawn up for the Chiefs of Staff on these lines, inviting them to consider the military implications of the two courses.[27]

Notable men in British public life took up in a more uninhibited manner the cry for military commitments. Lloyd George and Churchill in particular canvassed the idea vigorously. Both had close contacts with France, and they were disparaged in turn by Phipps, who assured French officials that neither man possessed much influence in Britain, and that their recommendations should be taken with a pinch of salt.[28] There was considerable validity in the Ambassador's criticism. Whether deservedly or not, Lloyd George was very widely distrusted; he had been out of office for fifteen years, and his age and political affiliations both made it exceedingly unlikely that he would ever return. Churchill appeared to some as an irresponsible, Puckish figure; to others as a tragic case of a brilliant young politician who had passed through a middle age of anticlimax.

First requirement of any scheme designed to contain Germany was a very close diplomatic alliance between Britain and France. Halifax soon came to doubt the attractions of the original French proposal, objecting to any 'further commitments unless [they] will not operate without our express concurrence at the time'. They would mean committing 'British foreign policy more or less blind to that of France'.[29]

What finally swept away any prospect of plans involving a definite British commitment was the report of the Chiefs of Staff.[30] The instructions eventually given to them were to examine the situation which would arise if a German attack on Czechoslovakia brought in Britain and France to the Czechs' support.

The situation prevailing in the west in the early spring of 1938 was very similar to that which had been projected for eighteen months later. The Allies, so the Chiefs of Staff argued, would be superior at sea, except in the Baltic; while initially the Germans would be superior on land and in the air. Britain's contribution at sea would be overwhelming, and her air forces considerably greater than those of France; but her land force would be piteously small. An army corps of two divisions, with supports, would be able to embark in a fortnight.

In the east, the prospects were gloomy in the extreme. There was much doubt whether Germany would need to take the field at all in order to overcome Czech opposition; for the vast bulk of Czech external trade needed to pass over German territory, and economic obstruction alone might well suffice to reduce Czechoslovakia to vassalage. If war came, Czechoslovakia had no power of sustained resistance. In the first phase of war, Germans would be expected to occupy Bohemia, including some of the armaments works which supplied not only Czechoslovakia but also her possible allies Yugoslavia and Romania. The Czechs would fall back on improvised defences in Moravia. Sir Thomas Inskip, Minister for Coordination of Defence, set a gloss on the Chiefs of Staff's report in even more depressing terms: 'It seemed certain that Germany could overrun the whole of Czechoslovakia in less than a week.'[31] The possibility of the Western Allies relieving pressure on the Czechs through diversionary activity was considered. A Rhine crossing to the south of Strasbourg would involve the invaders in difficult country; to the north there were strong German field defences. An air offensive was unlikely to produce great effect.

If Italy entered the war at once on Germany's side, this would set strains on the British navy in the Mediterranean and pose serious problems in the defence of Egypt. If Japan also entered the war on Germany's side, then the outlook was appalling. Various other European Powers might well be involved on one side or the other; but there was not much to suggest that their participation would radically affect the overall result. All allowance must be made for the political predilections of the Chiefs of Staff, who assuredly were not embued with any passionate desire to defend Czechoslovakia, democracy or the principles of the League of Nations; but their patriotism was not in doubt, and it is difficult to see how any other group of experts could have produced a fundamentally different assessment. The one thing clear beyond a shadow of doubt was that no war against Germany was by any means a certain 'walkover' for the Allies. At best, they could anticipate a long, tough war with a difficult victory at the end – very likely leaving Russia as the *tertius gaudens*. At worst they might easily go down in defeat, with the total ruin not merely of their authority in Europe but of their position throughout the world. It is interesting to reflect that the Chiefs of Staff at their gloomiest never approached the depths of pessimism and defeatism reached by Kingsley Martin, the very influential editor of the pro-Labour *New Statesman*, who 'felt that things had gone so far that to plan armed resistance to the dictators was useless. If there was a war we should lose it. We should therefore seek for the most peaceful means of letting them gradually get what they wanted.'[32]

Apart from the military risks involved, there were other questions. If the object of the possible war was merely to exclude Germany from the Sudetenland, many people were disposed to consider the game hardly worth the candle. 'I'm afraid', wrote Sir Alexander Cadogan, 'I can't look on the Reich's absorption of Germans with much horror. (Anyhow I don't believe for a moment that we're going to stop it.) I shan't be able to work up much moral indignation until Hitler interferes with other nationalities.'[33] Sir Thomas Inskip told the Cabinet Committee on Foreign Policy that Czechoslovakia was 'an unstable unit in Central Europe' – therefore, that he 'could see no reason why we should take any steps to maintain such a unit in being.'[34]

Chamberlain did not go as far as that. When the alarming military assessment dispelled his own hopes for a defensive alliance to protect Czechoslovakia, his predilection was in favour of an immediate and direct approach to Hitler. He would address the Führer in terms like these:

> Everyone is thinking that you are going to repeat the Austrian coup in Czechoslovakia. I know you say you aren't, but nobody believes you. The best thing you can do is to tell us exactly what you want for your Sudetendeutsch. If it is reasonable we will urge the Czechs to accept it and if they do you must give assurances that you will let them alone in future.[35]

Whatever arguments or ideas may have influenced certain minds, there can be no doubt that it was the report of the Chiefs of Staff which weighed most heavily on the Cabinet when they came to discuss Britain's policy in relation to Czechoslovakia on 22 March. Even the flat language of the official minutes leaves the reader in no doubt that they were profoundly shocked by the 'exceedingly melancholy document' – those were Halifax's words – which was set before them. The minutes record that 'Several members of the Cabinet, including the Prime Minister and the Foreign Secretary, admitted that they had approached the question with a bias in favour of some kind of guarantee to Czechoslovakia, but that the investigation . . . had changed their views.'[36] In the shadow of that document, the Cabinet decided

> to undertake no new commitment involving a risk of war; to endeavour to induce the Government of Czechoslovakia to apply themselves to producing a direct settlement with the Sudetendeutsch; to try and persuade the French Government to use their influence to forward such a settlement; and if circumstances should render this advisable to arrange for a joint or parallel approach by the British and French Governments to the German Government with a view to acceptance of any settlement that might be reached in Czechoslovakia.

Thus the Cabinet's object was to secure an internal settlement between the Czechoslovak Government and the Sudetendeutsch, rather than an international settlement between Germany and Czechoslovakia.

Loyal to his colleagues' decision, Chamberlain made an important and oft-quoted statement in the House of Commons on 24 March, in which he discussed with considerable frankness the problems confronting the British Government in relation to a possible commitment over Czechoslovakia. The Government, he declared, would not undertake a formal guarantee, but, 'When peace and war are concerned, legal obligations are not alone involved, and if war broke out it would be unlikely to be confined to those who have assumed such obligations. It would be quite impossible to say where it would end and what Governments might become involved.' By this formula he could hope on the one hand to warn Germany that Britain might be forced to intervene; yet, on the other hand, to leave Britain's hands to an extent free – and, more important, not to encourage the Czechs or the French in attitudes of unreasonable obduracy.

Britain, like everybody else in Europe, had been shaken from her moorings. In the course of a fortnight, not only had Austria ceased to exist, but practically all the fixed points on the map of Central and Eastern Europe had been called into question. Not a single frontier, not a single political system, could be considered secure. The structure which had been erected in the aftermath of the First World War, seemed ready to collapse. The Year of Munich had indeed begun.

3 Hopes and Fears

'If you do succeed in throwing any planks across the gulf, you will have done more for mankind than it is given to many to do.'   Halifax to Runciman, 18 August 1938. Runciman papers 296

Some of Neville Chamberlain's Cabinet colleagues – notably Oliver Stanley and Earl de la Warr – expressed fear that his statement to Parliament on 24 March had set the Anglo-French *entente* at serious risk.[1] This view was difficult to defend. The two countries had similar political systems which faced a similar threat from totalitarian Powers. They had a treaty of mutual defence against attack. Yet there was another even stronger link, which in the opinion of most people would have joined them inseparably in any event. As Viscount Halifax told the Cabinet Committee on Foreign Policy some days before the Prime Minister's speech, 'whatever might be the position under the Locarno Treaty, we in fact could not afford to see France destroyed, and we must therefore always come to her aid if she was attacked by Germany.'[2] Rather curiously, Halifax followed this statement with one which might seem difficult to reconcile with it. Provided no direct German attack were launched on France, 'We could in any particular case say whether we would or would not come to France's assistance. This had . . . a restraining effect both upon France and upon Germany.'[3] Perhaps Halifax was thinking of the unlikely possibility of a 'limited war'; perhaps he believed it was possible to bluff France and Germany simultaneously about Britain's practical commitment to the former. In either event, his stance seems strangely similar to that of Sir Edward Grey, immediately before the German invasion of Belgium in 1914. An argument existed for the view that – apart from treaty obligations – Britain had no inescapable bonds of interest with France. True or false, that argument was seldom put forward, and it was tacitly assumed by almost everybody that the two countries stood or fell together.

About a month after the *Anschluss*, the French 'Popular Front' Government collapsed. Phipps made no secret of his own delight at the event. Like all French Governments of the time, the succeeding administration would necessarily be a coalition of groups, and for a time there seemed a chance that the fiercely anti-Italian Paul-Boncour would remain at the Quai d'Orsay under the new Premier, Edouard Daladier. Phipps 'had Daladier and Paul Reynaud informed indirectly that it would be most unfortunate if Paul-Boncour were to remain.'[4] Halifax heartily approved of the Ambassador's intervention.[5] The choice alighted eventually upon Georges Bonnet. President Beneš of Czechoslovakia had good reason to hate Bonnet, but did not err far when he called the new Foreign Secretary, 'in the worst sense of the word, a typical politician'.[6] Phipps would have preferred to see Chautemps in the job, but Daladier's personal animosity towards Chautemps made that appointment impossible, and the Ambassador considered the eventual selection to be 'the semi-right thing'.

What obsessed British officials in their dealings with France during this period was the feeling that the French were encouraging the Czechs to live in a thoroughly unreal world, based on an illusion of Anglo-French power and prestige which had long vanished. On this view, Czechoslovakia was relying on the 1925 Treaty with France as an inviolable safeguard against German attack, and for that reason was not interested in reaching any settlement with the Sudetendeutsch: perhaps in the general hope that 'something might turn up', perhaps in the more specific hope that events would force Britain into the alliance, and concessions would be unnecessary. On 11 April, while the new French Government was being formed, Halifax sent instructions to Phipps which evinced considerable irritation:

> Unless the French and Czechoslovak Governments can be brought to face the realities of the present position it is to be feared that the Czechoslovak Government will not realise the necessity of making drastic concessions to the German minority but will content themselves with superficial measures which, though they might have been adequate in the past, will no longer meet the case.[7]

All this turned on the unstated presumption that Czech concessions would subserve the interests of peace. On that hypothesis, however, how could the two Governments be brought to face 'realities'?

If the intransigence of Beneš increased the danger of a German attack, then, on the face of it, Britain should presumably set what pressure she could upon the Czech President to advance 'reasonable' proposals. The real agony of the situation, from Britain's point of view, was seen most clearly by Cadogan: 'We should be taking an implied commitment to Beneš, and if his proposals were brushed aside by Hitler, we should be in a still more graceless position if we didn't support him.'[8] This, then, was Britain's dilemma: leave the Czechs to their own devices and Sudetendeutsch grievances will fester, therefore the danger of war will grow; alternatively, if Britain sets pressure on the Czechs she will gradually acquire a commitment to fight on their behalf if, in spite of her efforts, war should come about. Of course, there was always the possibility – as many people freely argued – that Germany had already made up her mind to secure control of Czechoslovakia as prelude to much wider plans; that the Sudetendeutsch were her excuse and not her reason; that no concessions by the Czechs could alter that situation. To that point we shall need to return repeatedly: suffice for the moment to say that neither world opinion, Empire opinion nor British opinion at home was as yet convinced that this was so, and any obvious intransigence by the Czechs in face of the undeniable Sudetendeutsch grievances would seriously decrease the measure of support should war follow. If the British Government and Parliament could suddenly have known the reality of Hitler's intentions in all its brutal horror, there was still singularly little they could do in relation to Czechoslovakia itself, save to attempt as unobtrusively and indirectly as possible to induce Beneš to offer concessions to the Sudetendeutsch which uncommitted folk would acclaim as 'reasonable'.

A plaintiff may be expected to state, not only the nature of his grievance, but also what redress he seeks. It was by no means clear for a long time just what redress the Sudetendeutsch desired. On this matter, the spokesman would presumably be their leader, Konrad Henlein. Early in April, a British consular report disclosed that 'during the past few weeks the majority of the Sudeten Germans has ceased to be even nominally loyal to the State as the [Sudeten Nazi] party leaders still profess to be.' It was 'openly declared that if Henlein is not prepared to adopt a radical policy he will be disowned and brushed aside.'[9] The movement was evidently of a 'grassroots' character; as Newton explained, 'It may well be true that the big industrialists will embrace National Socialism with reluctance. The real strength of the movement lies rather with the employees.'[10] This point was reinforced in May, when the local elections indicated that nearly 90 per cent of the German vote had gone to Nazi candidates in the Sudeten areas. No doubt the Reich Nazis were doing what they could to encourage disaffection among the Sudetendeutsch; but it would be profoundly misleading to ignore the spontaneous support which the separatist movement enjoyed.

Not until Henlein spoke at Karlsbad on 24 April were the Sudeten demands formally set down. Most important of these were autonomy for the Sudeten areas; full equality for Czechs and Germans within the State (which included proportional appointment to Government posts); removal of 'injustices' (which presumably meant mainly the provisions of the 1919 Land Reform Act) and reparation for their past effects; and, finally, 'full liberty to profess German nationality and German political philosophy'. Ostensibly at least, Henlein did not propose disruption of Czechoslovakia by inclusion of the Sudetenland within the Reich.

Diverse opinions existed as to whether the Sudetendeutsch would eventually seek this transfer; and judgements on that question did not always follow the line which the communicant's sympathy or antipathy towards Germany might suggest. Sir Nevile Henderson decided that the change would eventually be brought about by popular vote;[11] while Jan Masaryk, Czech Minister in London, decided that Henlein's own influence would operate the other way, though for somewhat cynical reasons: he 'would probably prefer to remain a great man in Czechoslovakia rather than a small man in Germany'.[12]

Soon after the Karlsbad speech, Henlein visited Britain. Initiative came from the Sudetendeutsch side, but the visit was encouraged by British Ministers.[13] He met a number of people with official posts, and also had a remarkable interview with two of the most powerful critics of Government policy, Winston Churchill and the Liberal leader Sir Archibald Sinclair. Henlein 'insisted, and offered to give his word of honour, that he had never received orders or even recommendations (*Weisungen*) from Berlin.'[14] Amplifying the points raised at Karlsbad, Henlein

> said that in his view there were three possibilities . . . autonomy within the Czechoslovak state . . . plebiscite probably leading to the Anschluss . . . war. His policy was to make a last attempt to arrive at agreement on some form of autonomy, but it must be reached soon, and by agreement, as his followers were impatient and undoubtedly at the moment would prefer an Anschluss.

Many people in Britain felt, or could easily be brought to feel, sympathy for the Sudetendeutsch. It is not astonishing that Henderson should complain of 'the folly of Versailles of including $3\frac{1}{2}$ million Germans in that Slav State'.[15] There was a remarkable discussion in the Cabinet as to whether Thomas Masaryk had ever wished for their inclusion, or whether they had actually been foisted upon the new Czechoslovakia by Lloyd George. Hankey, who was in a position to know, strongly denied that Lloyd George had done anything of the kind.[16] Traditionally, complaints against the 1919 boundaries had been raised most strongly on the left, among people who objected to the 'vindictive' character of the peace settlement and believed passionately in national self-determination. When it became apparent that transfer of the Sudetendland or even regional autonomy would mean the aggrandisement of Nazi Germany, most of the left fell silent on that question. There is an uncomfortable ring of truth in Sir Nevile Henderson's comment that if the Sudetendeutsch 'were Hungarians or Poles or Romanians or citizens of any small nation, all England would be on their side. They are Germans, so we shut our eyes to realities, and are influenced by other considerations, some honourable, some chivalrous, but many egoistical or inspired by fear.'[17] A few, even in the Labour Party, persisted embarrassingly in the old views of the left. In March 1938, a disturbing letter appeared in *The Times* over the signature of Lord Noel-Buxton, who had served in the 1929 Labour Cabinet, arguing for a plebiscite in the Sudetendland, to be followed by transfer of territory if the population so desired. Government reaction to the letter was perhaps indicated by the view of the Home Secretary, Sir Samuel Hoare, who concurred in a correspondent's opinion that the proposal was 'sheer insanity and even sabotage'.[18]

The Sudetendeutsch were not the only people in Czechoslovakia who were beginning to make autonomist claims. The Magyars, who in some districts formed a majority of the population, were also discontented. Slovak nationalists, even in Habsburg times, had not always favoured union with the Czechs, and the current Czech attitude towards them was curiously reminiscent of the Habsburg attitude towards the Czechs themselves. A Czech Civil Servant assured Newton that it was 'difficult for anyone not intimately associated with the Slovaks' to appreciate 'how backward and unbalanced they are. They live in their tiny villages completely under the influence of a fanatical priesthood.'[19] Whether that view be true or false, it is easy to appreciate that officials who held it did not always ingratiate themselves with the indigenous population. The Slovak People's Party, led by Father Hlinka, was an important force for Slovak separatism. In the 1935 General Election it had won twenty out of the fifty-nine parliamentary seats in Slovakia.[20] There were special problems in the even more backward Ruthenia, to which we shall return. Poles in Teschen had their own grounds of complaint as well. These 'nationalities' were unlikely to make serious trouble for the Prague Government of their own initiative, but would be likely to follow a lead from the Sudetendeutsch, or from interested outsiders.

Thus if Beneš and his colleagues really wished to remedy the grievances of the Sudetendeutsch, it is difficult to see how they could do it without virtually rebuilding the whole state from its foundations. The President was undeniably the 'strong man' of Czechoslovakia; but unfortunately he was widely distrusted by his political opponents and viewed with considerable suspicion by his international friends. During the late spring and summer of 1938, the suspicion grew in many places that Beneš and his colleagues lacked the will – even if they possessed the power – to make major concessions, and were trying to stall the Sudetendeutsch, the Reich Germans, the other minorities and the Western Democracies alike.

The political question whether Czechoslovakia was (or could become) a viable unit, and the moral question whether Britain should prepare to defend its territorial integrity if it be challenged from outside, were but two aspects of the problem. There was a third: the aspect which had stopped the British Cabinet in its tracks when they read the appraisal by their Chiefs of Staff in March. As Hankey reminded the Service advisers, 'A decision to make war was affected not merely by political but at least as much by military considerations.'[21] There was a marked tendency on the part of politicians and diplomats of all colours to allow these grim and mundane considerations to slip out of sight amid a welter of moral and political theory. That tendency was strongly marked in Britain: it was far more so in France.

The unrealism of French politicians was especially disturbing because of the growing fear that Britain might be compelled to underwrite French policies. In April, Halifax complained of the 'tendency not only in the Press but also in official quarters both in France and Czechoslovakia to give too broad an interpretation to the Prime Minister's statement'[22] – that is, to interpret Chamberlain's statement of 24 March to mean, not that Britain could possibly be brought into a war over Czechoslovakia, but that she would certainly participate on France's side. If French foreign policy was unrealistic to the point of folly, then the dangers for Britain were infinite. Some sort of top-level contact between the two Governments was imperative.

At the end of April, senior Ministers from both countries met in London. The position was discussed at length, but not resolved. Daladier, wrote Halifax, 'had spoken from the text that the military position . . . depended upon the political, whereas in the British view the political position was inevitably largely dependent on, and governed by, the military.'[23] British accounts of the meeting indicate that the French failed either to confute the British military assessment or to suggest how the situation could be radically improved in the future; while the French met a similar impasse when they tried to elicit a promise from the British that if Beneš could be brought 'to go a very long way to reach a settlement', Britain would then guarantee Czechoslovakia.

The discussions were certainly not particularly productive; but they nearly collapsed in circumstances which would have proved disastrous. Chamberlain's private account indicated that the talks

> came out all right in the end but they were pretty difficult. Fortunately the papers have had no hint of how near we came to a break over Czechoslovakia. By one o'clock on Friday we had reached a deadlock. Daladier was saying to his own people that it was no use going on and Léger, the Permanent Under-Secretary, told Vansittart that he had never been so dispirited over any conference.[24]

At least the parties remained in contact, and coordinated their actions as far as they could.

Then, for a time, there was a deceptive lull. In the middle of May, Chamberlain thought that foreign affairs were 'at the moment a bit easier', and felt that he had 'no reason to expect an immediate explosion at all'.[25] That optimistic opinion was reinforced a few days later when Newton, after a long interview with Beneš, reported the President's assurances that his Government was 'convinced of the necessity of coming to an agreement without delay'.[26] Beneš almost immediately found himself the target of a Manifesto in the Czechoslovak press, over the signatures of many intellectuals, enjoining the Government to stand firm. In spite of this Manifesto, Beneš continued in the path of moderate concessions to the Sudetendeutsch. On 19 May he announced that the Government had agreed to the principle of a 'Nationalities Statute'. Negotiations would be held between the interested parties, and would be followed by legislation.

The same evening, reports began to come in of German troop movements in the vicinity of the Czechoslovak frontier, and there were rumours that leave had been cancelled for Sunday 22 May, the day of

Czechoslovak communal elections. In the next couple of days, attitudes on both sides hardened. Sudeten Nazi meetings were broken up by Socialists and Communists; two Sudetendeutsch citizens were shot dead by a gendarme; and the Sudeten Party declared that they were unwilling to discuss the proposed Nationalities Statute until freedom of press and assembly were guaranteed and order restored. On 21 May the Czechs replied to the reported troop movements by ordering partial mobilisation. The following day, the British Cabinet heard of 'disquieting . . . reports that control was passing from the Government into the hands of the General Staff at Prague.'[27] The German Ambassador told Halifax of the danger of 'incidents' – adding that 'If, for example, 100 Germans were killed in some clash, it would be impossible for Germany not to take action.'[28]

There was some doubt as to whether the German troop movements which had sparked off the crisis had been any more than the ordinary seasonal movements in the area, or whether the Germans had had more sinister intentions. Chamberlain thought the latter, writing a few days later: 'The more I hear about last week the more I feel what a "d—d close run thing" it was. . . . I cannot doubt in my own mind (1) that the German Government made all preparations for a coup, (2) that in the end they decided after getting our warnings that the risks were too great . . .'[29] Whether that view was correct or not, it certainly looked to the world as if Germany had plotted aggression of some kind on Czechoslovakia, but had been held back either by the Czech mobilisation or by diplomatic intervention from the Western Democracies.

Whatever real injury German prestige had suffered, the newspapers of the West certainly gloried in the outcome. Rather mildly, Chamberlain wrote that 'It certainly was unfortunate from our point of view that the European press should have insisted on crowning us with laurels.[30] Henderson's judgement was often poor, but there may have been something in his contention that 'what Hitler could not stomach was the triumphant outcry of the foreign Press, and particularly the British, to which above all he is susceptible.'[31] This, argued the Ambassador, 'definitely put him on the side of the war party'.[32]

The effect of the crisis within Czechoslovakia itself was also severe. The British Military Attaché in Prague reported on his visit to the Sudetenland about a week after the acute danger had passed. Czechoslovak troops were 'at once feared, despised and hated': a somewhat astonishing observation, since units of the army were deliberately composed of a mixture of races. The Attaché's conclusion was that 'the Czech and German races in the Sudeten area are so fundamentally antagonistic to one another that it is almost impossible to visualise them pulling together under any conditions which the Czechs can accept.'[33] The Czechs were sorely tempted to derive the lesson that the Nazis – Sudeten or Reich German – had been bluffing, and their bluff had been called. If Czechoslovakia kept her nerve, there was nothing to fear. Why bother to make major concessions to the Sudetendeutsch, which could set the whole Czechoslovak state at risk? The Sudetendeutsch were likely to conclude that they were second-class citizens in an occupied country; that emancipation could only come from the Reich, so near to their own home. Yet Beneš had made his offer of negotiations in the direction of a Nationalities Statute. Whatever either side might think of the prospect of much good emerging from those negotiations, they must for the sake of appearances go through the motions of conferring. In that discouraging atmosphere negotiations between the Czechoslovak Government and the Sudetendeutsch leaders were inaugurated at the end of May.

Again the British press added an unnecessary aggravation to a tense and difficult situation. On 3 June Lord Noel-Buxton's plebiscite proposals were taken up editorially by *The Times*. As *The Times* was generally regarded abroad as a semi-official organ, this looked like a British Government kite, and placed Halifax in such a difficult position that he was compelled to authorise Newton to deny Government complicity.[34] The Foreign Secretary even wrote a private letter to Geoffrey Dawson, the Editor, in which he spelt out his own concern in the clearest possible terms. British efforts to promote a settlement within the existing frontiers of Czechoslovakia, explained Halifax,

> may be seriously compromised. Herr Henlein will be placed in an impossible position if he can be represented as agreeing to terms less favourable than those represented as reasonable by the 'Times', whilst Dr. Beneš for his part can hardly be expected to incur the responsibility . . . for reaching terms of settlement if they are only to be the stepping-stone to a plebiscite involving the break-up of his state.[35]

Halifax added a significant tailpiece: he did not preclude the possibility that 'it may be ultimately necessary to fall back on a plebiscite in order to forestall a worse catastrophe'. Dawson, however, disputed these remonstrances;[36] it will later be noted that this was not the last, nor the most serious, occasion on which *The Times* intervened in a similar way.

As summer advanced, prospects of an agreement diminished perceptibly. Newton had never been very sanguine about the chances that Beneš could persuade simultaneously the Czech public, the army and five political parties to make concessions which would also satisfy the Sudetendeutsch.[37] The Sudetendeutsch leaders, for their part, suspected that 'by a combination of apparent optimism in the Press and practical procrastination in the negotiations, Dr. Beneš hopes to exhaust the patience of the Sudeten negotiators so that they will break away and enable Dr. Beneš to place on them the blame for the ensuing rupture.'[38]

In the middle of June the British Government began to consider some possible initiative of its own in the matter. Halifax mentioned to the Cabinet Committee on Foreign Policy a suggestion that – in event of a breakdown – the British Government should 'offer the services of some distinguished person to act as mediator between the two sides.'[39] Possible names were mentioned to the meeting; a few days later Sir Horace Wilson, head of the Civil Service and personal *aide* to the Prime Minister, drew up a list for Halifax. The Foreign Secretary preferred Lord Macmillan, the famous Judge, but gave next place to Viscount Runciman.[40] What approach, if any, was made to Lord Macmillan is obscure; but Runciman was certainly interviewed by Halifax on 29 June.[41]

Runciman had served in Asquith's Liberal Government before the war; had sided with Asquith during the Liberal dissensions; had eventually become a Liberal National, and joined the National Government as President of the Board of Trade in 1931. In May 1937, when Chamberlain became Premier, Runciman was only offered junior Cabinet rank. He was deeply upset at the affront,[42] and withdrew from the Government with a Viscountcy. The middle of 1938 found Runciman at sixty-eight years of age in noticeably declining helath, and with his public career evidently at an end. Wilson thought that he was 'superficially not a model negotiator but capable of a crispness which again might turn out to be what was needed.'[43] The negotiator's role, as Halifax explained it to Runciman, 'would be that the Czech Government and the Sudeten leaders had, on the suggestion of H.M. Government, invited you to help them to reach an agreement within the framework of the present Czechoslovak state on the points still at issue between them.'[44]

If the leading Ministers had some reservations about Runciman, the proposed mediator had even deeper doubts about the task which was urged upon him.[45] Furthermore, the early breakdown of negotiations which Halifax had originally seen as a condition preceding British intervention, did not occur. By the middle of July, however, there was still no sign of a settlement, nor yet had Runciman given a final reply to the invitation. Some pressure was set upon him by Halifax,[46] who was at last able to inform Newton on 16 July that the offer had been accepted – subject to the stipulation 'that he [would] not be asked to proceed unless both sides agree[d] to receive him and to explain to him fully their respective points of view.'[47]

It proved by no means easy to persuade either side to accept the mediation. Newton's first report of Czech reactions was far from encouraging:

I conveyed suggestion for investigation and mediation to President Beneš today, 20 July. He seemed greatly taken aback and much upset, flushing slightly and hardly recovering his full equanimity by the end of a conversation which lasted over two hours . . . It would provoke a most serious crisis in his country and might entail resignation of the Government and even, he hinted very confidentially, his own.[48]

Czech objections were apparently overcome by a threat to publicise both the British offer and the Czech refusal. The French were told in good time and made no difficulties – but asked to be kept informed of the progress of negotiations.[49]

As for the Sudetendeutsch, it was more or less taken for granted that they would follow advice – or instructions – from the Reich. Henderson discovered from a confidential approach to the State Secretary (civil service head of the German Foreign Office) that his political superiors were unlikely to raise objections. Von Ribbentrop was at this time on holiday and allegedly unable to be contacted; the British did not in fact hear from him until they received a chilling letter more than three weeks later.[50] By a surely curious coincidence, Henlein and his deputy Frank were both also *incommunicado* in the latter part of July.

While negotiations were still in this delicate and preliminary stage a press leak appeared in the *News Chronicle* – perhaps because the news had passed through Paris, perhaps as a result of the close links which some of the newspaper's journalists had with Czechoslovakia. In spite of the fact that Runciman's own conditions had not yet been satisfied, the British Government thereupon resolved to make an immediate announcement, and Chamberlain told the Commons on 26 July of what became known as the 'Runciman Mission'. The Prime Minister explained Lord Runciman's terms of reference: he 'would not be an arbitrator but investigator and mediator . . . independent of His Majesty's Government and of all Governments. He would act only in a personal capacity and it would be necessary that he should have all facilities and information placed at his disposal.'

All the same, it was impossible to deny that the British Government was deeply involved in the success or failure of the mission. Newspapers which usually looked at Czechoslovak questions from very different angles from each other shared a considerable feeling of doubt and hesitation. The *Evening Standard* wondered 'whether the British Government should ever have persuaded the Czech Government to assent to the appointment – on terms so capable of being misunderstood, and for a purpose so fraught with complications.'[51] The *News Chronicle* was rather more forthright: 'No-one – certainly no Czech and no German – is going to accept Mr. Chamberlain's bland assurance that the British Government has really nothing to do with his success or failure.'[52]

The mediator himself had deep doubts, though on different grounds. Before he even embarked on the mission, Runciman wrote reflectively to Chamberlain: ' . . . But what a cockpit Bohemia has always been! For 800 years they have quarrelled and fought. Only one king kept them at peace, Charles V, and he was a Frenchman! How then can we succeed?'[53]

When the Runciman Mission arrived in Prague, first impressions were not propitious. On about 4 August, Runciman reported that Beneš 'does not show much sign of an understanding or respect for the Germans in Czechoslovakia'.[54] Several days later he asked Halifax rhetorically,

'Where are we going? The answer can be given as well by you as by me. Success depends on whether or not the Führer wants to go to war. If he does the excuse will be found easily.'[55] More wistfully, he added: 'It is a pathetic side of the present crisis that the common people here, and I am told everywhere, are looking to me and my mission as the only hope of an established peace. Alas, they do not realise how weak are our sanctions, and I dread the moment when they find that nothing can save them.'

On 17 August the talks apparently reached deadlock. The following day Halifax discussed the situation in a long and rambling letter to Runciman; he decided that an admission of failure 'would probably by reaction precipitate an acute crisis and might tempt the German Government to immediate action'.[56] The very time at which the deadlock had occured seemed balefully significant. As early as mid-July Halifax had warned the Cabinet of 'disquieting hints to the effect that Germany was working up for a rapid *coup* at the end of August'.[57] Observations from men with as disparate views as Vansittart and Henderson had pointed to a resolution of the dispute one way or another in August or September.[58] The breakdown could well presage the final crisis which might lead to war.

It proved a false alarm. Runciman was able to bring the parties together again, and talks were resumed on 24 August. The following day, the Runciman Mission reported confidentially that the Czechs were prepared to make proposals not far from the Karlsbad points; three autonomous Sudeten districts would be set up, from which Czech police would be removed; while Czech and German officials would be exchanged.[59]

Henderson saw this development as a greatly opportunity. Runciman, he urged, should report to the British Government 'what he intends to recommend to Czech Government as basis for negotiation, say, Swiss cantonal autonomy'.[60] The British Government, proposed the Ambassador, should urge the French to inform their Czech clients that unless the proposal was accepted they would be left to their fate; while, simultaneously, Britain should tell Germany that if she used force to upset such a solution, Britain would regard that as a *casus belli*. Vansittart was delighted to hear that view from such a source: 'Sir N. Henderson has at last found out that the only thing Germany will, or ever does, understand is force. R.V.'[61]

This strange concurrence between Henderson and Vansittart was, however, based on a fundamental misapprehension. Sir Orme Sargent had seen a fortnight earlier that the widespread view that Runciman would promulgate a solution was fallacious: 'This to my mind would be in the nature of an arbitral award, and the one thing that Lord Runciman made it clear that he was not going to do was to act as arbitrator.'[62] In various ways, the Foreign Office sought to induce Runciman to intervene actively in the dispute. F. Ashton-Gwatkin, who had been seconded from the Foreign Office to assist the mission, persuaded himself that Runciman would make 'some pronouncement in hopeful terms' before Hitler made his anticipated major statement of policy at Nuremberg on 12 September.[63] He and other Foreign Office officials suggested that Runciman should attempt to see Hitler, to dissuade him from making any pronouncement at Nuremberg which could wreck the negotiations.[64] Another member of the mission, R. J. Stopford, argued to the opposite effect: such intervention would probably be resented by Czechoslovakia, and might well commit Britain to war if the attempt were made, but failed.[65] Runciman, probably wisely, decided to adhere to his original terms of reference.

Then the recent hopes of a settlement suddenly receded. This time even Vansittart was disposed to set blame on Beneš rather than the Germans. The Czech President, he told Jan Masaryk, 'so far from wishing to discuss his new proposals was retreating from his original intention to give the Sudetens as much as the public opinion of the world would expect Czechoslovakia to give.'[66] At the beginning of September Runciman and Newton on separate occasions told Beneš 'that if the British people had to choose between Henlein's Karlsbad eight points and war, there is no doubt as to the decision.'[67]

Even the supple Beneš could manoeuvre no longer. On 6 September he communicated to the Sudeten leaders the so-called 'Fourth Plan'. The Czech Government was prepared to reconstitute the country on a cantonal basis; would grant protection to the national minorities; would ensure that State employees were recruited in proportion to the numbers of the various races and that public works and government orders were similarly apportioned: language equality would be recognised. Virtually, these were the Karlsbad points.

Runciman, for once, was sanguine, considering the new proposals to form a 'satisfactory basis for negotiations'.[68] The Sudeten Party's legal adviser recommended acceptance. A couple of days before, Henlein had informed a member of the Runciman Mission that he preferred autonomy within Czechoslovakia to incorporation in the Reich. Even Henlein's deputy Frank, generally considered to be more extreme in his views, had told a British M.P. the same thing a few weeks earlier.[69] No doubt any features of the Fourth Plan which still did not meet Sudeten requirements were negotiable.

Ever since March, British policy had been based on the notion that it was possible to secure an 'internal settlement' within Czechoslovakia between the Government and the Sudetendeutsch. In the teeth of the most immense difficulties from every possible side, this had apparently been achieved, largely through the work of Viscount Runciman. All that remained was to work out the details. If the various parties meant approximately what they said, then surely there was real hope of lasting peace in Europe.

4 Moment of Truth

'L'opinion anglaise en général, aussi bien que celle, dit-on, du Cabinet, parait encore partagée entre deux tendances: l'une demandant que l'on soutienne le Tchécoslovaquie contre le bluff agressif du Reich hitlérien, l'autre préconisant un compromis pour éviter de redoutables complications pouvant entraîner la guerre.' *Le Temps*, 19 September 1938

'Veracity is not, I regret to say, the strongest point of the average French politician.' Sir Eric Phipps to Halifax, 17 September 1938 (copy). PHPP 1/20 fo. 86

During the hiatus in Czech-Sudeten negotiations at the end of August, there were many signs that a major international crisis was brewing. British statesmen were conscious of a serious risk that the whole of Europe, including the United Kingdom, would be at war within a few weeks. On 27 August Sir John Simon, Chancellor of the Exchequer, spoke at Lanark. He reaffirmed the position Chamberlain had declared in the House of Commons on 24 March, and particularly the Prime Minister's broad hint that a war involving France was likely to bring in Britain as well. The *News Chronicle* wrote that the speech 'has been received with satisfaction almost everywhere but in Berlin'.[1] Unfortunately, this was the one place in the world where reactions really mattered, and a day or two later Vansittart noted emphatically that the speech 'has had no effect at all on the German War Party'.[2]

On 30 August a Meeting of Ministers was held. This was for all practical purposes a Cabinet Meeting: the first time the Cabinet had been called together for five weeks. Added importance derived from the presence of Sir Nevile Henderson, who was specially invited. Chamberlain noted that 'the crisis atmosphere was unmistakably present'.[3] Needless to say, this 'crisis atmosphere' was encouraged by the press; on the morning of the meeting, Chamberlain found it necessary to send a note to Halifax urging him to warn people at the Foreign Office to be careful what they said to journalists.[4] The Ministers needed to decide whether some clearer definition of British policy was now necessary, in view of the growing urgency of the Czechoslovak situation.

Several general propositions were spelt out at the Meeting of Ministers, apparently without dissent from those present. They are significant not because they really added much to the situation, but because they throw light on how thoughts were running at the time. No new threat should be issued, the Ministers concurred, unless Britain proposed to carry it out; and if such a threat were issued it could not possibly be kept secret. If war came, there was nothing Britain, France or Russia could do to prevent Czechoslovakia being overrun; and, whatever the result of the war, it was unlikely that the country could be reconstituted in its present form. Furthermore, as Chamberlain put it somewhat pointedly, 'War in present conditions was not . . . a prospect the Defence Ministers would view with great confidence.'[5]

Most of these points were made repeatedly in the days and weeks which followed. Another observation advanced by the Prime Minister perhaps failed to register sufficiently either on contemporary critics or subsequent writers: 'Supposing the threat were made, and had the desired results on this occasion, would that be the end of the story? The steps taken on the 21st. May had not proved the end of the story . . .'

Vansittart had for some time been impressing on Halifax the idea that a note should be sent to Germany, to the effect that if she intervened by force Britain would at once declare war.[6] This view did not find universal favour among the Ministers; but Halifax came very close to saying that if France was involved, Britain would be bound to follow. This went perceptibly further than Chamberlain went in March, or Simon a few days before the meeting. Halifax also asserted, apparently without challenge, that 'there was much more in the present crisis than the attempt to defend Czechoslovakia against Germany. We were in effect concerned with the attempt of the dictator countries to attain their ends by force.' The final conclusion, however, was somewhat lame: Germany should be 'kept guessing'. Vansittart's comment afterwards was pungent: 'The policy of "keeping Germany guessing" is the policy that obtained in 1914. We did keep Germany guessing, and they ended by guessing wrong, and war followed.'[7] Chamberlain evinced a different kind of concern at the dangerous game of diplomatic poker which seemed to be developing. 'While the F.O. keeps repeating that we must "keep Hitler guessing", that is exactly what he does to us and we have no definite knowledge of his intentions'.[8]

These widespread apprehensions abated for a moment when Beneš told the Sudeten leaders of his 'Fourth Plan' on 6 September, and the following day announced it to the world. By a disastrous accident, on the very morning of the general announcement *The Times* carried a long editorial, containing one crucial sentence:

. . . It might be worth while for the Czechoslovak Government to consider whether they should exclude altogether the project, which has found favour in some quarters, of making Czechoslovakia a more homogeneous state by the secession of that fringe of alien populations who are contiguous to the nation with which they are united by race.

With some understatement, Halifax described that editorial as 'unhappy'. Runciman, with similar moderation, observed that it 'has added to my difficulties'. Even a man as closely cognisant of British diplomatic practice as the Liberal Viscount Samuel, suspected that it had been a kite from the British Government.[9] So did the French Foreign Secretary. The Czechs, who obviously had similar suspicions, instructed their Minister in London to enter formal representations, while the Russian Ambassador declared that it would have 'the worst possible effect' – an opinion with which Halifax concurred. Yet in truth all suspicions that it had been inspired by the Government were quite unfounded. Dawson, the Editor, 'had had the article written on his own responsibility entirely, but had been prompted to it by a suggestion from a British ex-Ambassador, who was convinced that that was the only solution.'[10] The Conservative *Daily Telegraph*, which feared lest the leader reflected 'the views of persons in high positions in this country', and the Liberal *News Chronicle*, which thought the leader had 'encouraged German extremists . . . and . . . engendered a corresponding defeatism in Prague',[11] both approved of the Labour Party's demand for an immediate recall of Parliament.

The damage had been done, and was irreparable. Halifax issued his denials on the day the editorial appeared. It was not easy to discover whether the Germans believed those denials or not; but, in any event, the Nazis could scarcely be accused of adopting an unreasonable attitude if they repeated a proposal with such impeccable credentials. The day of the *Times* editorial brought other news which may have been related to that expression of opinion. The Sudetendeutsch leaders took the excuse of a not particularly dramatic incident at Mährisch-Ostrau (Moravska Ostrava) to suspend negotiations with the Czech Government. Even then, the possibility of a settlement was not formally abandoned. Sudetendeutsch demands arising out of the incident were conceded, and discussions were resumed on 10 September.

About this time, the British Government received information which indicated that Hitler proposed to march into Czechoslovakia on some date between 18 and 29 September. Although the Ministers had agreed that no formal warning be delivered to Germany, this piece of news, conjoined with the other bad tidings, set things in a different context. On 9 September Chamberlain, Halifax and Simon met, and decided on a rather serious admonitory message, which Henderson should deliver in Berlin. The Ambassador, fearing the effect of any 'repetition of 21 May', urged strongly that the *démarche* should not be made. The Government's point, however, was put in a rather more oblique manner. The British Director of Naval Intelligence told the German Naval Attaché that 'everybody in England knew that if France were involved in war we should be likewise'. The Attaché was reported to have been 'greatly shaken'.[12]

It is relevant to ask why the British Government was so circumspect in issuing a warning of this kind. It was generally believed that the Führer was 'possibly or even probably mad' – Halifax's words to the Cabinet.[13] In such circumstances, a 'warning in the nature of an ultimatum . . . might well have the effect of driving Herr Hitler over the edge'. A great deal of British diplomatic behaviour was governed by the notion that Hitler was a dangerous lunatic, who would be liable to encompass the destruction of himself and everyone else if crossed, yet who might behave in a rational and even generous manner if treated sympathetically.

Hitler's speech of 12 September said surprisingly little that was new. There was a cryptic indication that he 'would not suffer the oppression of the Sudeten Germans'; but the real importance of the speech lay not so much in what was said as in the events which supervened upon it. That night, huge crowds assembled in the Sudeten towns of Eger and Karlsbad. Police fired, killing half a dozen people and injuring many more. On the next day, martial law was proclaimed in the affected area. Lord Runciman described the *dénouement*.

As a result of the bloodshed and disturbance thus caused, the Sudeten delegation refused to meet the Czech authorities, as had been arranged on September 13th. Herr Henlein and Herr Frank prepared a new series of demands – withdrawal of State police, limitation of troops to their military duties, etc., which the Czechoslovak Government were again prepared to accept, on the sole condition that a representative of the Party came to Prague to discuss how order should be maintained. On the night of September 13th, this condition was refused by Herr Henlein, and all negotiations were completely broken off.[14]

In theory, Henlein still did not treat this as a final rupture. On the following day, 14 September, he declared that now 'the eight Karlsbad points would in no way suffice, but account would have to be taken of the Sudeten German right of self-determination'.[15] If the Karsbad points were not the Sudeten Party's demands, then it was difficult to see what those demands were; and if Beneš had not realised them, it was difficult to see what 'realisation' meant. It is just possible that the Sudetendeutsch leaders had been telling the truth when they declared a short time before that they would prefer living in a 'cantonal' Czechoslovakia to living in Germany. This point was sublimely unimportant, for the Sudetendeutsch leaders had been thrust aside by the march of events. Nobody in the world cared what Henlein or Frank thought or said, save in so far as they could be regarded as the mouthpieces of Hitler. To remove any remaining doubts, Henlein himself made a final statement on 15 September, declaring that cooperation between Czechs and Sudetendeutsch had proved impossible, and concluding 'Wir wollen ins Reich' – 'We want to go over to Germany'[16]

The duties of the Runciman Mission were at an end. It had been called into existence to mediate between the Prague Government and the Sudetendeutsch. The dispute was now not internal but international in character: between Czechoslovakia and her possible allies on one side and Germany on the other. Any further mediation must be performed with the authority of a major Government, not by a private individual.

Thus by the middle of September 1938 there was a patent danger of almost immediate war. How would the British people react to such an event? The substantive issue of the Sudetenland had been a matter of intense controversy for months. The criticisms of those who attacked the Government for being weak are familiar enough; but it is important to recall that some important voices were raised very much the other way. Lord Rothermere, proprietor of the *Daily Mail*, wrote a sulphurous article in his newspaper on 18 July, headed 'How long shall the Czechs imperil peace?' Rothermere described the Czechs as 'the petty bullies of Central Europe', and concluded, 'If Czechoslovakia becomes involved in war, the British nation will say to the Prime Minister with one voice – "Keep out of it!"' This was an extreme, and perhaps rare, view. Much more moderately, J. L. Garvin wrote in the *Observer*, 'There is nothing in the world more abhorrent to [the British public] than the thought of being dragged into war now or ever for the sake of one race against another in the racial confusion of Czechoslovakia.'[17] Sir Philip Gibbs, writing to *The Times*, described Czechoslovakia as 'an artificial state which reproduces in a small area all the mixture of races in the old Austro-Hungarian Empire' – adding, 'Within 24 hours of war Czechoslovakia would have disappeared off the map and Europe would be fighting to the death for a non-existent state which was a violation of all racial ideals.[18] Such opinions were by no means confined to the political 'far right'. J. A. Hobson expressed a rather unorthodox Liberal view in the *Manchester Guardian*: 'No one can detest the Hitler rule more than I do, but I am not prepared to promote a general war in order to prevent by force the Sudeten Germans from exercising their ordinary right of self-determination.'[19] The attitude of the Labour peer, Lord Noel-Buxton, has already been noted; it was reasserted on a number of occasions in letters to the press during 1938. In September, Sir Nevile Henderson met John McGovern, one of the 'far-left' I.L.P. M.P.s, whom the Ambassador wrongly thought to be a Communist. McGovern's views were thus reported:

> He astonished me by his reasonableness: all for self-determination, not a bit impressed by Krofta – [Czechoslovak Foreign Secretary], didn't see why the Czechs should rule over anybody but Czechs or Slovaks, and very perturbed over Soviet Communist influence, which he described as endeavouring to create a second Spain in Central Europe.[20]

On the other side, the T.U.C. expressed a more common Labour view when it declared, at its annual Conference in September, that 'The British Government must leave no doubt in the mind of the German Government that they will unite with the French and Soviet Governments to resist any attack on Czechoslovakia.'[21] This view was similar to Winston

Churchill's call for a 'Grand Alliance'. Sir Bernard Pares, the great diplomat, saw the issue virtually as a classic power-struggle. He concluded that 'little support' would be given to the view that Britain should stand aside while France was beaten – however unwise France's 1925 alliances might have been. He perceived strong parallels with 1914: 'At that time Serbia stood in the way of a free run for the German powers to the Aegean and the East. Now it is Czechoslovakia.'[22]

The agony of decision, which in its own way faced everybody in the land who tried to reach some kind of conclusion, was perhaps stated most clearly by Anthony Crossley, Conservative M.P., but a severe critic of the Government's foreign policy: 'The usual rhetorical question runs, "Are you willing to fight for Czechoslovakia?" and invites the answer "No.". . . The wider question ought to be propounded in this form: "Are you prepared to contemplate a Germany which dominates Europe and masters its resources from the North Sea to the Black Sea?" '[23] For most people, who made no pretence to understand the various military, ethnic and diplomatic aspects of the question, everything seems to have turned on this issue of judgement: whether Hitler's objective was the domination of Europe or not. Nevertheless, there was a very important consideration which Halifax suggested to the Meeting of Ministers and later to the French Ambassador, which could not fail to have wide attraction: 'A certain war today to avoid an uncertain one tomorrow never appealed to him.'[24] People who thought, on balance, that war would arrive sooner or later, might therefore be willing to support policies designed to avert an immediate war.

The British Government could not rely on a docile press to educate public opinion in the direction it desired. The Opposition press spoke with something like unanimity for resistance to Hitler, even at risk of war. Newspapers which were widely regarded as supporters of the Government were deeply split. *The Times* would probably follow most closely the Cabinet's line: but the astonishing way in which it could embarrass the Government has already been noted. The *Daily Mail* and its associate the *Evening News* were spokesmen of Lord Rothermere; the *Daily* and *Sunday Express*, and the *Evening Standard*, of Lord Beaverbrook. Both proprietors were exceedingly reluctant to support any policy involving risks of immediate war – though, half way through September, Lord Beaverbrook did plead successfully with Chamberlain for a Minister to be designated to deal with the press:[25] adding, 'They are all anxious to follow you'. Yet undoubted differences persisted. The *Daily Telegraph* leaned on the side of resistance to Hitler, and provided the chief platform for those Conservatives who felt the same; the *Yorkshire Post* was, if anything, even more strongly committed the same way.

Hitler's Nuremburg declaration of support for the Sudetendeutsch, followed so swiftly by the breakdown of Czech–Sudeten negotiations, led to the general view that unless the Sudetenland were ceded to Germany, orders to march would be given. Czechoslovakia had avowed her intention to resist; France that she would stand by the Czechs; Russia that she would fight if France did; Britain, while avoiding a formal commitment, had implied the same thing. Was it possible that some at least of these statements by the five countries concerned contained an element of deliberate bluff – or, even if they were really meant at face value, that some accommodation might be reached? It was difficult to believe that any of the states concerned would incur the horrors and dangers of war consciously and deliberately for the sole purpose of determining the political location of three and a half million central Europeans. Yet it was credible that war might arise 'by accident', or because questions of pride rather than interest were deeply engaged.

France – if she cared to assert her position – was really the key to the situation. The Czechs were unlikely to go to war unless they could feel tolerably certain of French support. Britain would certainly not go to war unless France did so. Russia had no obligation to fight unless France did.

The French Prime Minister repeatedly asserted that his country would stand by Czechoslovakia. On 8 September 'Daladier declared most positively that, if German troops cross the Czechoslovak frontier, the French will march to a man . . . not for *les beaux yeux* of the Czechs but for their own skins, as, given time, Germany would, with enormously increased strength, turn upon France.'[26] A couple of days later, the French Ambassador in London said the same thing. Halifax hinted at the possible advantages of that policy which had been advanced so imprudently in *The Times* a few days earlier. For the first time he 'threw out the idea of some form of voting by the SDs, and said it would be silly to fight a war to prevent that. Corbin's only reply to all this was to say "Czechoslovakia today, France tomorrow".'[27] The reasons given by both Frenchmen, as well as the emphatic character of their declarations, seemed to permit little doubt as to France's intentions.

Yet on the same day as the French Ambassador in London was interviewing the British Foreign Secretary, the British Ambassador in Paris met the French Foreign Secretary. In the formal interview Bonnet told Phipps that 'the French Government would accept and support any plan for a settlement of the Sudeten problem that either His Majesty's Government or Lord Runciman might put forward.'[28] The less formal parts of the meeting revealed an even more anxious Bonnet, and Phipps concluded, 'My impression is that Bonnet, perhaps more than Daladier, and certainly more than Mandel, Reynaud and Co., is definitely anxious for a possible way out of this *impasse* without being *obliged* to fight.'[29] On 13 September Phipps again saw Bonnet. The French Foreign Secretary was reported to the British Cabinet as being 'in a state of collapse'. According to the account they received, the American Colonel Lindbergh had told the French Government that Germany possessed 8,000 aeroplanes and could produce 1,500 more a month.[30] Lindbergh may have been misquoted; but Bonnet told Phipps, 'We cannot sacrifice ten million men in order to prevent $3\frac{1}{2}$ million Sudetens joining the Reich. M. Bonnet said that the French Government would prefer a federal and neutralised Czechoslovakia with autonomous Sudetens inside it, but in the last resort . . . would consent to plebiscite.'[31] According to this account, Bonnet had become so panic-striken that Phipps felt bound to exercise considerable care in conversation with Daladier 'not to give away M. Bonnet, for if they are of different opinions this might have led to a Cabinet crisis with deplorable results.'[32]

Perhaps this caution was unnecessary; for when Phipps saw the French Prime Minister the same day he reported: 'M. Daladier of today was quite a different one to the M. Daladier of September 8, and tone and language were very different indeed . . . I fear French have been bluffing, although I have constantly pointed out that one cannot bluff Hitler.'[33] Daladier had an unfortunate reputation in his own country as 'un taureau à cornes de limaçon'[34] – 'a bull with horns of a snail' – but by this time Mandel was the only member of the French Cabinet whom Phipps was disposed to characterise as a 'possible warmonger'.[35] 'Everything', wrote Sir Thomas Inskip in his diary, 'showed that the French didn't want to fight, were not fit to fight, and wouldn't fight.'[36]

The Foreign Secretary had felt very similar suspicions about the French for a long time. Early in August, Halifax wrote to Henderson:

. . . Supposing the worst happens. The French will presumably mobilise – unless indeed the Czechs have so behaved as to warrant the French saying they have been eminently unreasonable and therefore doing nothing. I should doubt (a) the French attacking the Siegfried Line, (b) the Germans attacking France, and in one form or another I should have guessed there would have been talking.[37]

It would surely be the ultimate absurdity if France declared war on the Czechs' behalf, and then – as soon as the Czechs had sustained their swift and inevitable defeat – concluded peace again, without French and German armies being engaged at all.

In apparent contrast with the French, diplomatic officials of the Soviet Union took every available opportunity to affirm in the most emphatic terms that they would honour their treaty obligations to Czechoslovakia. Yet there was very little contact between Britain and Russia on the matter. Ivan Maisky, Soviet Ambassador in London, constantly complained in sympathetic ears that Britain 'wished to keep them at arm's length',[38] and there was 'no single conversation with the Soviet Foreign Office during the whole period of crisis'.[39] Yet the medal had another side. The position had not radically changed from when Chilston reported to Chamberlain on the side-effects of Stalin's purges. In the Prime Minister's account, 'Russians are now afraid to come near [Chilston]. As a result he gets no information and the condition of this country is a mystery to him. He never sees Stalin nor does anyone of his colleagues.'[40]

In such circumstances the British had no means of confirming Soviet Government assertions, and were bound to treat them all with great suspicion. Chilston's view, in September 1938, was that

> If the Soviet Government intervened on behalf of Czechoslovakia, this would at the outside, be limited to sending some of their own forces to assist the Czechs, and possibly to operating submarines against German ships in the Baltic. As regards land forces he thought they would at most concentrate troops on their western frontier.[41]

In the summary of Lord Chilston's views preserved in the Foreign Office papers there is a minuted comment that they 'are generally borne out by other information in the possession of the Foreign Office.' Vansittart, who had persistently urged that Russia should be brought into arrangements for the defence of Czechoslovakia, quoted the view that Russian aid to the Czechs might amount to the supply of a hundred aeroplanes – adding, 'But that would be a very small factor'.[42]

Such information about the likely actions of France and the Soviet Union in event of war was well known to the Government, but was for the most part unknown, even unsuspected, by the Government's critics. On 17 September Chamberlain and Halifax had a very frank talk with Sir Walter Citrine, Hugh Dalton and Herbert Morrison, who came as delegates from the National Council of Labour. When Chamberlain told the delegates that 'he himself did not think France would come in' – adding that 'the French have only twenty-one aeroplanes equal to German aeroplanes and they have only five hundred altogether', Dalton remarked 'that it was, then, very reckless of M. Daladier to have made the declarations that he had made, for they have completely misled many people'.[43] When Chamberlain went on to report a conversation Beneš had had with Litvinov 'from which it was clear that, though they might raise the matter at Geneva, Russia was not likely to do anything that was effective', the three Labour delegates 'were obviously very astonished at this, and were still more so when Lord Halifax pointed out that this information about Russia had been confirmed by our Ambassador at Moscow as well as by our own General Staff.' Dalton confessed that the recent declaration of the Labour Party had been based on the notion that 'they were backing France and Russia. It now seemed that they were misled by pronouncements made on behalf of those two countries.' This account must be treated with the caution which should always be given to *ex parte* reports, but it was not designed for circulation, and there was no point in presenting it in a slanted manner. The Labour delegates were obviously far better informed about military and diplomatic questions than most of the Government's critics; yet their misunderstanding of fact was profound. They, in their turn, were certainly not free to tell a wide circle of the Labour Party the most appalling facts which had been revealed to them, although the Ministers did leave it to their discretion how much they should say. Many of the differences of judgement about the Government's behaviour in the September crisis surely derive from the widely different assumptions of fact which different people made.

Just as there were massive doubts about the reliability and value of possible allies, so also was there enormous uncertainty about the long-term designs of Germany. Henderson thought that anything which went beyond the incorporation of German populations within the Reich, and the acquisition of overseas colonies, 'is, in fact, not only hypothetical but contrary to Hitler's own doctrine of nationality and of a pure German race.[44]

In order to form his own assessment of the situation, Chamberlain decided to operate what he called 'Plan Z'. The plan, as originally conceived, had been devised late in August, and the early initiates were Chamberlain, Halifax, Simon and Sir Horace Wilson.[45] It appears to have sprung entirely from Chamberlain himself. Halifax, when he first heard it, found the idea 'so unconventional and daring that it rather took his breath away.'[46] Henderson 'thought that it might save the situation at the eleventh hour.'

The original Plan Z was that at some critical moment Chamberlain should appear suddenly and unannounced in Berlin, and there demand an interview with Hitler. The Prime Minister would try to discover what Hitler really did want – and then, if the demand was tolerable, would discuss how it might be realised. If time permitted, Henderson should be alerted and authorised to inform von Ribbentrop. Everything depended on the element of complete surprise, and the appeal which it would make to Hitler's sense of the dramatic. Henderson persuaded Chamberlain to modify Plan Z to the extent that Hitler should receive prior notice of the Premier's visit[47] – for there was some apprehension lest the Führer should develop a diplomatic cold. Thus the meeting was not to resemble Cleopatra's apparition before Julius Caesar. Vansittart, however – who viewed the whole project with unfeigned horror – drew the even more baleful parallel with the Emperor Henry IV's humiliating visit to Canossa.[48] Sir Thomas Inskip, who heard of the proposal before it was raised in Cabinet, was tepid, but thought it would do no harm.

Runciman was also made privy to Plan Z. He had been cast for a very important role. Chamberlain meditated suggesting to Hitler that Runciman might act as final arbitrator between Germany and Czechoslovakia. With the greatest reluctance, Runciman agreed.[49]

Events moved swiftly. After Hitler's Nuremberg speech and the ensuing Sudeten disturbances came the gloomy reports of French opinion which finally decided Chamberlain to set the scheme in motion.[50] Plan Z was launched on the night of 13 September;[51] the following morning the Prime Minister sought ratification from the Cabinet. The only Minister who seems to have had any hesitation at all was Walter Elliot, Minister of Health.[52]

Daladier had made an alternative proposal to the British Government: that Runciman should publish his own plan, and a three-Power Conference be arranged – France, of course, being the third. Runciman, as has been noted, did not consider the time had come for publishing any plan. Everyone seems to have agreed that Chamberlain's proposal was the better, and it finally received emphatic approval.

Before the Prime Minister's visit could profitably be made, it was necessary to consider some matters which were likely to be raised, and their implications. Hitler would certainly refuse to accede to any settlement which did not involve transfer of the Sudetenland to Germany. This point was more or less tacitly accepted by the Cabinet: the most truculent view was that of Duff Cooper, who argued that 'the choice was not between a war and a plebiscite but between war now and war later'. 'Plebiscite' and 'transfer' for the Sudetenland were generally considered to mean, in practice, the same thing. Even Cooper does not seem in the end to have stood out against the majority.

The immediate difficulty over any transfer of the Sudetenland was to persuade the Czechs to accept it. The only possible inducement Britain could hold out to the Czechs was herself to guarantee the truncated remains of the country. Chamberlain told his colleagues that 'he was most unwilling to accept' this idea, but it was 'the only answer which he could find'. Thus, in spite of all the arguments which had been advanced during the previous six months, the Cabinet now found itself contemplating the first guarantee which Britain had ever given to anybody in Central Europe: and a guarantee, furthermore, which Britain knew and everybody else knew could never achieve its ostensible object if it were implemented. At best, it would be a nominal *casus belli* for British participation in a general war. No immediate Cabinet decision was needed; but it was useful to raise the matter at that point. The Führer accepted Chamberlain's offer with alacrity. Phipps was left with the somewhat embarrassing task of explaining everything to the French. Daladier 'did not look very pleased'; but Bonnet, whom the Ambassador saw later, apparently had no reservations.[53]

If the press is any guide – and on this matter it probably is – British approval was well-nigh universal. Labour's *Daily Herald* headlined the news, 'Good luck, Chamberlain!' and was convinced that his 'bold course . . . will receive general support'. The Liberal *News Chronicle* commended 'one of the boldest and most dramatic strokes in modern diplomatic history'. The 'rebel' Conservative *Daily Telegraph* – using the word 'appeasement' in its older sense – promised that 'the good wishes of everybody who has the appeasement of Europe at heart will accompany Mr. Neville Chamberlain on his mission'.[54] Secure in this universal approbation, Chamberlain departed to meet Hitler at Berchtesgaden.

Politicians and public alike tended to blot from their minds any serious consideration of what was likely to happen when he got there.

Chamberlain had a fairly clear idea of what he proposed to say, and had sent a letter to Runciman a few days before the Cabinet meeting, explaining his intentions. The Prime Minister proposed to urge Hitler 'that he had an unequalled opportunity of raising his own prestige and fulfilling what he had so often declared to be his aim, namely the establishment of an Anglo-German understanding, preceded by a settlement of the Czech question.'[55] The Prime Minister would then go on to suggest that Runciman should be invited to act as arbitrator in the dispute.

Events followed a different course. The two leaders met at Berchtesgaden, with only an interpreter present.[56] Hitler, wrote the Prime Minister, 'showed no signs of insanity but many of excitement'. At an early stage of the discussions, the Führer launched into a diatribe about the recent Sudeten disturbances in which, he declared, three hundred Germans had been killed. This was a wild exaggeration of an undoubtedly serious incident, and Chamberlain was, of course, in a position to know the general facts of the case. Hitler gave every appearance of believing the Nazi propaganda story himself. 'The thing', he declared, 'has got to be settled at once . . . and I am prepared to risk a world war rather than allow this to drag on.' As to the fate of the rest of Czechoslovakia, Hitler considered that 'if Sudeten Germans come into the Reich then the Hungarian minority would secede, the Polish minority would secede, the Slovak minority would secede – and what was left would be so small that he would not bother his head about it.'

Chamberlain, who could be a great deal tougher than some of his critics imagined, turned at bay. 'I replied, "If the Führer intended to settle this matter by force without waiting even for a discussion between ourselves to take place, what did he let me come here for? I have wasted my time."' This, in the Prime Minister's view, 'was perhaps the turning point of the conversation. Herr Hitler became quieter in his manner.' Chamberlain's account goes on: 'He said, "Well, if the British Government were prepared to accept the idea of secession in principle and say so, there might be a chance then to have a talk."' Chamberlain replied that he was in no position to commit the British Government, still less the French; but, in his purely personal view, he 'had nothing to say against the secession of the Sudeten Germans from the rest of Czechoslovakia, provided that the practical difficulties could be overcome'. At the end of the meeting, an arrangement was concluded between the two men. Hitler would try to hold back his military machine, but would guarantee nothing should further serious incidents occur. Chamberlain would consult his colleagues, and the two leaders would meet again.

On 17 September Chamberlain reported back to the Cabinet. The crisis, in his view, had lifted somewhat. 'The situation when he went to Germany', he told them, 'had been one of desperate urgency. If he had not gone he thought that hostilities would have started by now.'[57] The Prime Minister gave a clear lead to his colleagues. He 'had formed the view that Herr Hitler's objectives were strictly limited'. On the basis of that conviction, he recommended them to accept the necessity to cede the Sudetenland, and discuss how this might be brought about without conflict.

Viscount Runciman, who was invited to that Cabinet meeting, threw significant light on Sudeten attitudes. In his view, the parties had come close to a solution within the ambit of the original functions of his Mission, earlier that month; yet the situation had now radically changed, and the Sudetendeutsch would no longer accept any arrangement which left them within the frontiers of Czechoslovakia.

On the substantive question before them as to whether to do what lay in their power to expedite transfer of the Sudetenland from Czechoslovakia to Germany, the Cabinet was profoundly divided. Some members were willing that the cession should be made, apparently without reference to whether Hitler had reached the end of his European aims or not. Viscount Hailsham, Lord President of the Council, thought that it was in Britain's interest to prevent any Power dominating Europe, 'but that had now come to pass and he thought we had no alternative but to submit to what [one colleague] regarded as humiliation.' The Lord Chancellor, Viscount Maugham, also accepted the need to let Hitler have his way – though, in his view, 'except for some possible loss of prestige, British interests were not involved'. Sir Thomas Inskip, Minister for Coordination of Defence and another eminent lawyer, considered that war should be averted because the likely upshot was 'changes in the state of Europe which might be satisfactory to no one except Russia and the Bolsheviks'. Different as these three approaches were from each other, none of those Ministers suggested – as Chamberlain did – that the Sudetenland must represent the limit of major concession to Hitler in Europe; or that the Sudetenland should be ceded because, on balance, the arrangement was the best for those immediately concerned.

Four other members of the Cabinet took views which balanced those of the lawyers. Duff Cooper was as emphatic as he had been three days earlier in mistrust of Hitler. It was 'difficult to believe that the self-determination of the Sudeten Germans was Hitler's last aim' – indeed, 'there was no chance of peace in Europe so long as there was a Nazi régime in Germany.' Earl de la Warr, the Lord Privy Seal, was anxious for some *quid pro quo* from Hitler – otherwise 'it was doubtful whether the Government could carry this policy in the House of Commons or in the country and that we should do irreparable damage to our prestige'. Oliver Stanley, President of the Board of Trade, was prepared to accept the need for a Sudetenland plebiscite, yet advanced an argument which seems totally inconsistent with his conclusion: 'This is not the last of Hitler's coups. The present Nazi régime could not exist without coups. The present was a better rather than

1 German Ambassador von Ribbentrop with Viscount Halifax, as the latter departs for Germany, November 1937. (*Radio Times Hulton Picture Library*)

THE LIMIT

Herren Hitler and Henlein (to Dr. Beneš). "There! Now we can all chat together comfortably."

2 Czech-Sudeten negotiations. The talks had just collapsed when this cartoon was published, 14 September 1938. (*Reproduced by permission of Punch*)

3 British diplomats Sir Eric Phipps (left) and Sir Nevile Henderson leaving the Foreign Office. (*Radio Times Hulton Picture Library*)

4 Viscount and Viscountess Runciman prepare to depart for Prague, 2 August 1938. (*Radio Times Hulton Picture Library*)

5 French representatives in London, 26 September 1938. Left to right: Georges Bonnet; Edouard Daladier; General Gamelin. (*Radio Times Hulton Picture Library*)

6 French reaction to Munich: crowds cheer Edouard Daladier at Le Bourget. *(Radio Times Hulton Picture Library)*

7 The visit to Rome, January 1939. Left to right: Ciano; Halifax; Chamberlain; Mussolini. (*Radio Times Hulton Picture Library*)

8 Germany seizes Prague, March 1939: the head of the procession of occupying troops. (*Radio Times Hulton Picture Library*)

a worse time to fight . . . Six months or a year hence . . . Germany's difficulties would have largely disappeared.' Earl Winterton, Chancellor of the Duchy of Lancaster, 'thought [Hailsham's] arguments could equally be used to justify acquiescence in the invasion of Kent or the surrender of the Isle of Wight.' Winterton had written earlier to Halifax, threatening two or three Cabinet resignations if the plebiscite were forced on the Czechs; but nothing was said at Cabinet about that suggestion.[58]

In this deeply divided Cabinet, Chamberlain found himself in a more or less central position: always the most comfortable location for a Prime Minister to occupy. He stood between the very pacifist view of the lawyers and the truculence of Cooper and his friends who foresaw further trouble in the future. It was quite clear that cession of the Sudetenland really did represent the absolute limit of what was generally tolerable to British opinion: anything more would split the Government as well as the country. Certainly the total dismemberment of Czechoslovakia, at which Hitler had hinted at Berchtesgaden, would be intolerable to a substantial section of the Cabinet.

Here the Ministers were back at the problem which they had confronted in a more hypothetical manner a few days earlier: how to bring the Czechs to accept the need to surrender the Sudetenland. The only feasible solution implied concessions at both extremes in the Cabinet. Cooper's friends must concede the need to surrender the territory; Hailsham's friends must concede the need to issue guarantees which could lead to war at a later date; Chamberlain and Halifax both gave support to the view that the deal should be made; but the Cabinet was not invited to take a formal decision.

A further question arose. If the Sudetenland was to be transferred, how should the transfer be effected? People had often spoken of a plebiscite; but was a plebiscite either necessary or wise? Nobody really doubted how the Sudetendeutsch would vote. A few districts were of mixed population, but in most of the important places there was a clear majority. Plebiscites would spark off similar demands by Hungary and Poland, perhaps by Slovak separatists as well. Whoever occupied the mixed areas during plebiscite, the charged atmosphere was likely to generate disturbances which could easily vitiate agreement. The prevailing Cabinet view was that plebiscite was an unsatisfactory device, and it would be far better to effect any transfer of territory through some kind of top-level agreement.

The British Cabinet could go no further without discussions with the French. As Vansittart pointed out to Halifax, 'All we know definitely as to the attitude of the French Government is really as to the attitude of Bonnet. We do not know much about Daladier . . . and as to the attitude of all the rest of the French Cabinet we know really nothing.'[59] There were signs that France was aggrieved at being omitted from the discussions; and there was obvious need for the two Western Democracies to hammer out an agreed policy before Chamberlain again met Hitler.

Senior members of the two Governments met in London the following day, Sunday 18 September. The account of their deliberations which was published a few years after the war, in the official *Documents on British Foreign Policy*, perhaps leaves the reader in some doubt as to why busy Ministers of two countries in the teeth of an intense crisis found it necessary to prolong discussions from the morning until after midnight. A more revealing account, however, was given by Chamberlain to the Cabinet next day.[60] Chamberlain told the Ministers from the two countries what had passed at Berchtesgaden: adding that unless the Sudetenland was transferred, 'we must expect that Herr Hitler's reply would be to give the order to march'. Chamberlain found that 'the darkest hour was before lunch'; but during lunch a series of confidential talks took place. Daladier told Chamberlain that he considered Beneš could be brought to agree to cession of the Sudetenland, but the 'general principle of self-determination' would raise more serious difficulties. Bonnet told Halifax that everything turned on whether Britain would 'join in some form of international guarantee of Czechoslovakia'. When the formal meetings resumed, the Ministers completely concurred that the plebiscite idea would prove disastrous: as Daladier put it, it would 'plunge all Europe into chaos'. The French Prime Minister now pressed the need for a British guarantee, as the sole hope of persuading the Czech Government to cede the Sudetenland. The British demurred, but would 'not exclude consideration' of the suggestion. That was not enough for Daladier. 'It would be useless to offer to consider the proposition. Furthermore, the French Government were not prepared to urge upon the Czechoslovak Government the acceptance of the proposals under discussion unless that Government were given some security.' At Berchtesgaden, Hitler had made much of the argument that Czechoslovakia, possessing a military alliance with France and Russia, was a 'spearhead at his flank'. With such alliances subsisting, a British guarantee entailed great risks, which weighed heavily on Halifax. He swung round, however, when the proposal emerged that Czechoslovakia should become a neutral state: that is, it should receive guarantees from other Powers, but should not be authorised to give reciprocal undertakings to others.

After much further discussion, the Ministers agreed to attempt a settlement on these lines. But nothing was certain. Neither the British nor the French Ministers could be sure that they would carry their own Cabinets without disastrous splits. It was even less certain that the Czechoslovak Government would accept; less certain still that the proposed plan would satisfy Hitler. Finally, there remained various dangers which none of the four Governments could accurately foresee: a coup by the Czech army; a major 'incident'; intervention by Poland or Hungary. Only if every single fragile link in the chain held was there any chance of preserving peace.

5 On the Precipice

'May God keeps us out of war for the Sudeten! If the Germans are going to behave as the Winston Churchills of this world believe, we shall have lots of opportunities later for going to war with them. Let us reserve our efforts for a cause which will be 100% just and not one based on emotions of fear and hatred or even of false reason and false prudence.'   Sir Nevile Henderson to Sir Alexander Cadogan, 30 March 1938 (copy). FO 800/269 fo. 71 seq.

On the morning of Monday 19 September the British Cabinet again met. They were far from happy about the proposed guarantee to Czechoslovakia. Innumerable difficulties were raised. What obligations would the guarantee entail? What other countries would give guarantees as well? Would the guarantee be 'joint' (which meant that it would only take effect if every single guarantor was prepared to uphold it) – or would it be 'several' (in which case Britain could conceivably find herself one day compelled to defend Czechoslovakia alone)? Would it affect the integrity of Czechoslovakia in respect of claims by Hungary and Poland? One useful feature of the situation, from the point of view of Chamberlain and Halifax, was that those Ministers who most feared to give a guarantee because it might lead to a future war were also the ones who were most acutely apprehensive of an immediate war – which, as they all knew full well, only a guarantee could avert. Record of the discussion does leave the reader with the impression that most Ministers were very clear about what they were guaranteeing, or upon what terms.

Simon probably clinched the argument.

The French Ministers on arrival had been somewhat woebegone, but they had gone away with heart and courage restored to them by the Prime Minister. At the same time, any lingering fear that he might have had, that the attitude of this country might have operated to prevent the French Government from fulfilling their obligations had been entirely dispelled by Sunday's meeting.

The general recommendations of the leading Ministers were agreed. Halifax had warned the Cabinet earlier that Daladier had been 'very doubtful of the attitude of two or three members of his Government', but during the meeting the satisfactory news came through that the French Council of Ministers – who were conferring at the same time – had agreed to ratify the decisions of the previous day.

Again the press introduced a further hazard into an exceedingly tense and dangerous situation. The French newspapers reported the gist of the highly confidential discussions between the two Governments. At least one experienced British diplomat concluded that the effect of these revelations would be to make Hitler increase his demands still further.[1] His guess was probably not far wrong. The Berlin newspapers immediately proceeded to 'tell the Prague Government that their choice is between acceptance of the Anglo-French proposals and the destruction of their state.'[2]

There were other reactions of a very different kind. The National Council of Labour promptly adopted a resolution, asserting 'that this is a shameful betrayal of a peaceful and democratic people and constitutes a dangerous precedent for the future', and resolved to commence a great campaign of public meetings.[3] Sir Archibald Sinclair, in one of his most impressive speeches, reminded the Liberal Party Council that 'we have merely submitted to Herr Hitler's demands and our submission has been extracted, not by a sudden conversion to the justice of his case, but by the threat of war'. Viscount Cecil, son of a former Conservative Prime Minister, said practically the same thing.[4] Anthony Eden declared at Stratford-upon-Avon that 'The British people know that a stand must be made. They pray that it will not be made too late.' The *News Chronicle* wrote that 'bewilderment is giving place to a feeling of indignation'. Bitterly and angrily, the *Daily Herald* declared that the Czechs had been 'betrayed and deserted by those who had given every assurance that there should be no dismemberment of their country.' The *Daily Telegraph* warned that 'a policy which does not command general approval is worse than useless'.[5] Vyvyan Adams, most rebellious of the Conservative backbenchers, wrote to the same newspaper that 'the betrayal of Czechoslovakia will . . . stimulate the Nazi Government to such arrogance that it will some day commit an act of aggression which even France or Great Britain or both will deem intolerable, and it will make abundantly more probable our defeat in isolation.'[6] On 22 September, the *News Chronicle*, whose readership probably represented a wider spectrum of political opinion than that of any other element of the popular press, printed a page of letters on the subject, declaring that 'They are but a small fraction of the mass of correspondence almost unprecedented in volume and overwhelmingly opposed to the Anglo-French plan to partition Czechoslovakia.' The same night 'ten thousand people massed in Whitehall . . . shouting "Stand by the Czechs!" "Chamberlain must go!" '[7] As in 1914, the vociferous section of 'public opinion' appears to have been a great deal more bellicose than the Government, and may well have exerted a considerable influence upon so-called 'leaders'.

The other side was not without its arguments. Lord Noel-Buxton chose *The Times* as the medium through which to embarrass and challenge his Labour colleagues: 'Those who oppose the Franco-British solution of the Sudeten problem may fairly be asked to discriminate as to what it is that they condemn. Few of them are ready to avow that they would prefer war now to possible war later on.'[8] There was also force in the less dignified comment of the *Evening Standard*: 'With every step taken by Mr. Chamberlain to preserve peace the moral idealists in the community become more bellicose. As the danger of war recedes they insist loudly that we should have been willing to fight.'[9] It is not difficult to see that the nation was profoundly divided, and that the divisions certainly did not always run along the ordinary lines of political cleavage. As usually happens in times of great crisis, we know much of the views of statesmen, of journalists, and of those who felt strong political commitments; we know little of the 'silent majority'.

The Government was deluged with opinions; but one comment which they invited may have been more influential than most of the unsought political and even diplomatic assessments. General Ismay sent a 'service' view, which was communicated to Inskip and Wilson on 20 September. He was asked to comment on the relative military advantages of immediate war and war six months later. His reply was brief and lucid. At sea, where considerable advantage lay with the Allies, this advantage would be reduced, though not destroyed, by postponement, since Germany would become more self-sufficient and therefore less amenable to the effects of naval blockade. On land, too, delay would on the whole operate in the enemy's favour. In the air, however, the balance of advantage lay completely the other way. Germany had a great lead over the Allies in air striking power. If war were delayed,

> It is open to us, provided that we make the necessary effort, to catch her up, or at least greatly reduce her lead, in the matter of defence (both active and passive) against air attack. By so doing we shall have heavily insured ourselves against the greatest danger to which we are at present exposed: indeed, by substantially reducing Germany's only chance of a rapid decision, we shall have produced a strong deterrent against making the attempt.

Then come the conclusion: 'It follows, therefore, that from a military point of view, time is in our favour, and that, if war with Germany has to come, it would be better to fight her in say 6−12 months' time than to accept the present challenge.'[10]

Meanwhile, the French set to work to coerce Czechoslovakia. British information indicated that the Czechs asked their allies point-blank whether they proposed to hold to their agreement if the Germans attacked. Evidently the French reply was more or less what the Czechs had feared. When Newton assured Beneš that Czechoslovakia was receiving, in return for compliance, 'a new and important guarantee by His Majesty's Government', the President retorted with some bitterness that the 'guarantee which he already possessed had proved worthless'.[11]

The Czechs had two more cards to play. In 1926 they had concluded a treaty with Germany, whereby the two countries engaged to submit future disputes to arbitration. The Czechoslovak Government now declared in confidence that they proposed to reject the Anglo-French proposals and invoke the Arbitration Treaty. Halifax instructed Newton to join with his French colleague in Prague to 'urge the Czech Government to withdraw this reply and urgently consider an alternative that takes account of realities'—otherwise Chamberlain would cancel his impending meeting with Hitler, and 'we could take no responsibility' for the ensuing situation.[12]

Another move was made by Czechoslovakia which was apparently not known (though it may have been suspected) in British diplomatic circles at the time. The Soviet treaty obligations were undeniably contingent on French action; but the Czechs asked Alexandrovsky, Soviet Minister in Prague, what would happen if Czechoslovakia fought and France defaulted on her obligations. Would the Russians help? The reply was that the Soviet Union would urge Czechoslovakia immediately to raise the matter before the League of Nations; if the majority of the League condemned Germany, even though the decision was not unanimous, Russia would go to Czechoslovakia's aid. This was not enough for Beneš; he explained that it would involve delay, and Czech morale was likely to collapse before any help was given. The reply was now returned that it would be enough for Russia if Czechoslovakia lodged her complaint at Geneva, and informed the Soviet Union. Beneš probed further and asked, in effect, whether Soviet assistance would be similar to that which they had given to the Spanish Republic. Alexandrovsky had 'received no instructions' and could not answer. The Czechs decided that the Soviet offer was not sufficient protection for their country.[13]

Although the Czech reply had still not been received, the British Cabinet met on Wednesday 21 September. By then, several new complications had been introduced into the crisis: or rather, problems which had been latent for some time were becoming acute. The second meeting between Chamberlain and Hitler had been scheduled for the following day, and the Führer was very anxious to have the arrangement finalised. At some risk that the Czechs might not deliver an acceptable answer, the arrangements were confirmed.

There was disturbing evidence of pressure which Hungary and Poland were mounting to secure redress for their respective grievances. The evidence, it is true, was only circumstantial, but it was considerable. The Hungarian Ambassador had already visited Halifax; the Polish Ambassador was about to do so. There had been mysterious comings and goings of Polish and Hungarian officials at Berchtesgaden; and there was news that both countries were taking military measures along their frontiers with Czechoslovakia. Angrily, Sir Samuel Hoare told the Cabinet that he 'had very little sympathy with the claims now being put forward by Hungary and Poland. Before the War no nation had treated their minorities worse than the Magyars, and since the War none had treated

their minorities worse than the Poles.'[14] We are not told what evidence
Hoare gave for this astonishing statement, but in any event, the Hungarian
and Polish claims were much better than that: Teschen, to which the Poles
laid claim, had itself been seized by Czechoslovakia at the time of Poland's
mortal peril in 1919; and the inclusion of a large Magyar area in the
Czechoslovak state was difficult to defend on any principle more elevated
than *vae victis*; but there was apparent danger of a concerted plan by
Germany, Hungary and Poland for the dismemberment of Czechoslovakia. All this seemed to confirm to the hilt the assessment which
Vansittart had written several weeks earlier: 'Hitler is not going to war
with the object of rectifying the Sudetendeutsch grievances or even with
the limited object of annexing the Sudetendeutsch districts. I have always
said that his object is to annex Bohemia and Moravia as well, so as to
disrupt entirely the Czechoslovak state.'[15]

If, however, the German design was no more than Hitler had suggested
to Chamberlain – to bring the Sudetendeutsch within the Reich and
remove the military threat of the 'spear at his flank', then there was no need
for war. Many people, including Vansittart and some members of the
Cabinet, had made it clear that they did not believe that interpretation for
a moment.[16] Yet, even on the 'Vansittart' view, it was still possible that
Chamberlain's proposal would hold back the Germans from future designs
on 'what is left of the unfortunate Czech state'. The official Cabinet
minutes leave the impression that most Ministers were far from convinced
either way.

In the course of the Cabinet meeting, a telegram was received from
Prague and communicated to the Ministers, indicating that the
Czechoslovak Government would accept fully the Anglo-French proposals
'on the supposition that the two Governments would not tolerate a
German invasion of Czechoslovak territory, which would remain
Czechoslovakian until the transfer had been accepted.'[17]

In such an atmosphere, Neville Chamberlain met Hitler at Godesberg
on 22 September.[18] The Premier could tell the Führer that the British,
French and Czechoslovak Governments had agreed in principle to cede
the Sudetenland. To meet Hitler's 'spearhead' argument, the three
countries were prepared to accept neutralisation of what remained of
Czechoslovakia, which would then receive guarantees from the Western
Democracies. As to the mechanism of effecting the transfer of territory,
Chamberlain recommended outright cession of indubitably German
districts, while a Commission should determine the fate of those areas
whose population was mixed.

Hitler demurred, arguing that the Hungarians, Poles and Slovaks also
found the existing situation intolerable. Two new arguments were put
forward. In the first place, 'people of the streets were being mobilised, and
the Bolsheviks were threatening to take the rudder'. Second, there had
been a great movement of Germans from out of the Sudetenland since

1918: 480,000, declared Hitler, of whom over 103,000 had left during the period of the current troubles.

Chamberlain would go no further.

He had induced his colleagues, the French and the Czechs to agree to the principle of self-determination: he had recognised the basis of the German claim and the fact that it was not possible to expect the Sudetens to remain as citizens of Czechoslovakia; in fact he had got exactly what the Führer wanted without the expenditure of a drop of German blood. In so doing he had been obliged to take his political life into his hands. As an illustration of the difficulties he had had to face, he mentioned that when he undertook his first flight to Germany he was applauded by public opinion. Today he was accused of selling the Czechs, yielding to the dictators, capitulating and so on. He had actually been booed on his departure today. Herr Hitler interjected that he had only been booed by the left, and the Prime Minister replied that he did not mind what the left thought, but that his serious difficulties came from the people in his own party, some of whom had actually written to protest to him against his policy.[19]

For the rest of the day, discussion between the two men was largely dialectical. Chamberlain, seeking a clear definition of the points at issue, sent a written document to Hitler. This evidently annoyed the Führer, who replied with a written memorandum, setting out the German demands. This document was examined by Sir Nevile Henderson and Sir Horace Wilson: men who certainly could not be considered hostile to conciliation with Germany. This gave more force to their reaction. According to the account which Chamberlain presented to the Cabinet, they

> informed the Prime Minister that it was an outrageous document, expressed in the most peremptory terms, and demanding that the evacuation of the Sudeten German area by Czechoslovak troops and police should start on Monday the 26th. September and should be completed a day or two later. The Prime Minister had thereupon said that, if this was the nature of the Memorandum, there was nothing for him to do.

Fragments of information which emerged from Godesberg during this phase of the meeting were so alarming that messages were sent to the Dominions, hinting that total collapse of the talks was likely.[20] With some difficulty, Chamberlain brought Hitler to extend the date of evacuation to 1 October, and to tone down the phraseology. About the only further concession which Hitler volunteered to Czech – or world – opinion was that he undertook to withdraw German troops during the actual period of plebiscite.

While Chamberlain was closeted with the Führer, there were altercations among Government members and supporters in Britain which gave considerable substance to the Prime Minister's observations about difficulties in his own party. Duff Cooper and Oliver Stanley wrote anxious letters to Halifax, to the effect that German troops should in no circumstances be allowed to enter Czechoslovakia until the frontier had been defined: otherwise 'they would inevitably overrun the whole country'.[21] Another letter was drawn up for Halifax, over the signatures of eight Government backbenchers, including Harold Macmillan, Robert Boothby and A.P.Herbert. Any concession beyond those already agreed would, they declared, 'be resented in the country . . . To embark upon it would be to court disaster.'[22] Meanwhile, the Czechs ordered full mobilisation of all classes of men up to forty years of age.

On 24 September, the British Cabinet commenced a two-day discussion of the German demands. By this time Chamberlain had formed a fairly definite view of Hitler's character and motives. As he told his colleagues,

> Herr Hitler has a narrow mind and was violently prejudiced on certain subjects, but he would not deliberately deceive a man whom he respected and with whom he had been in negotiation, and he was sure that Herr Hitler felt some respect for him . . . In the present instance Herr Hitler had said that if the principle of self-determination was accepted he would carry it out . . . He did not believe that Herr Hitler thought that he was departing in any way from the spirit of what he had agreed to at Berchtesgaden. [He was] sure that Herr Hitler was extremely anxious to secure the friendship of Great Britain. The crucial question was whether Herr Hitler was speaking the truth when he said that he regarded the Sudeten question as a racial question which must be settled, and that the object of his policy was racial unity and not the domination of Europe. Much depends on the answer to that question. The Prime Minister believed that Herr Hitler was speaking the truth.[23]

Chamberlain, however, 'hoped . . . that his colleagues would not think that he was making any attempt to disguise the fact that, if we now possessed a superior force to Germany, we should probably be considering these proposals in a very different spirit.'

As is frequently the case when exceedingly unpalatable decisions need to be taken, discussion in the Cabinet was discursive. There is little reason for thinking that Chamberlain's colleagues shared the Premier's delusions about Hitler's integrity; but the merit or otherwise of his substantive proposals did not necessarily depend on what people thought of the Führer's personal qualities. The real issue was whether the British Government should 'recommend' the Czechs to accept the German memorandum; though there was much doubt whether the Czechs would accede even if so.

The most dramatic episode of the Cabinet discussion was Halifax's account of his own mental anguish. On the second day he told his colleagues that

Yesterday he had felt that the difference between acceptance of the principle of last Sunday's proposal and the scheme now put forward a week later for its application did not involve a new acceptance of principle. He was not quite sure, however, that he still held that view. What made him hesitate was that it might be held that there was a distinction in principle between orderly and disorderly transfer . . . he could not rid his mind of the fact that Herr Hitler had given us nothing and that he was dictating terms, just as though he had won a war but without having to fight . . . The Foreign Secretary concluded by saying that he had worked most closely with the Prime Minister throughout the long crisis. He was not quite sure that their minds were still altogether at one.[24]

. . . Et tu, Brute! This was evidently the occasion on which Chamberlain passed an anguished note to Halifax:

Your complete change of view since I saw you last night is a horrible blow to me, but of course you must form your opinions for yourself. It remains, however, to see what the French say – if they say they will go in, thereby dragging us in, I do not think I will accept responsibility for the decision. But I don't want to anticipate what has not yet arisen. N.C.[25]

Viscount Hailsham, who a week or two earlier had been inclined to compound with the Germans, this time regaled the Cabinet with abundant evidence of Hitler's past mendacity, and spoke strongly against any pressure being applied to secure Czech compliance. Sir Samuel Hoare gave the weight of his own formidable authority in the same sense. Duff Cooper's views were predictably extreme: 'When Herr Hitler's present terms were published, there would be an explosion of public opinion . . . The revulsion of public opinion would lead to a defeat of the Government in Parliament, with far-reaching consequences.' Several other Ministers evidently thought on broadly similar lines. Having talked themselves to a standstill, the Cabinet finally agreed to reserve their decision until after a meeting with the French.

The French Council of Ministers also suddenly bristled, and showed a very different spirit from that suggested in some of the earlier reports from Paris. By a strange accident, they did not receive the text of Hitler's revised memorandum until the morning of 26 September, and they appear to have been considerably confused as to the nature of the proposals. Their unanimous view, however, was that 'it was no longer a question of reaching a fair agreement. Herr Hitler's object was to destroy Czechoslovakia and to dominate Europe.'[26] This – by implication – the French Council of Ministers would not tolerate; yet some people still felt doubt about their resolution. Dalton asked Jan Masaryk whether he thought the British and French Governments were 'getting a little more firm'. Masaryk's reply was neither diplomatic nor polite, but very explicit: 'Firm! About as firm as the erection of an old man of seventy!'[27]

The same evening, leading members of the two Governments met in London to attempt the very difficult task of hammering out a joint policy. Daladier was emphatic that the Godesberg memorandum could not be urged upon the Czechs, and that France would go to their aid if necessary. Sir John Simon then proceeded to treat Daladier in a manner closely redolent of Counsel interrogating an honourable but hostile witness. He sought, without success, to discover whether France proposed to launch an attack on Germany, or merely to retire to defensive positions behind the Maginot Line. Then Daladier swung to the attack. Did the British Government accept Hitler's plan? Would they press it upon the Czechs? It was not for Britain or France, but for the Czechs, to accept or reject the plan, replied Chamberlain. As for the second question, we were in no position to set pressure on the Czechs. Yes, replied Daladier, but does the British Government think that France should take no action? That is not for us to say, retorted the Prime Minister – but it is important for Britain to know what France intends to do.

Stalemate. The French Government either could not, or would not, say whether they proposed to make a real attack upon Germany which would draw off pressure from the Czechs before they were overwhelmed. Very likely the French military leaders, knowing well what happened to State secrets in France, were keeping the answer to themselves. Britain could hardly decide how to act until she was seized of this information; while the French could be excused for reluctance in disclosing what they knew to the British until they were reasonably sure whether Britain would fight or not. If that was how matters stood between the Western Allies, how much greater was the uncertainty about Czechoslovakia, and about Russia! Yet, by common consent, any or all of the four countries might well be at war with Germany within a week. Perhaps Western statesmen might derive some wry consolation from the thought that Germany was probably feeling similar doubts at that moment about Italy, Poland and Hungary.

Events, however, appeared to be taking charge. The Czechs were strongly disposed to reject the German memorandum. Whether this attitude could have been overborne by the united insistence of Britain and France is doubtful; but without that insistence there was no question of the Czechs having second thoughts on the matter. It was impossible to bring the Cabinets of the Western Democracies to insist on acceptance, although there were some individual members who would have been prepared to do so. Once the memorandum was refused, the German army would march and the Czechs would fight. Britain, France and perhaps Russia too, would very likely be pitched into war at Czechoslovakia's side.

Half an hour before midnight on 25 September, just after the French Ministers had departed, the British Cabinet met again. Chamberlain's determination to preserve peace if there was any possible way of so doing did not desert him; nor did his resourcefulness. The Prime Minister proposed to write a personal letter to Hitler, warning him that the Czechs would probably reject the memorandum, but proposing the appointment of an International Commission – containing German, Czech and British members – which would consider how to effect the transfer of territory which had already been agreed in principle, 'in an orderly manner, and as quickly as possible, and without shocking public opinion'.[28] The letter should be conveyed to the Führer by Sir Horace Wilson and Sir Nevile Henderson. In the last resort,

> If the letter failed to secure any response from Herr Hitler, Sir Horace Wilson should be authorised to give a personal message from the Prime Minister to the effect that if this appeal was refused, France would go to war, and that if that happened it seemed certain that we should be drawn in.

The French, of course, would be kept informed of all this. These substantive proposals were then accepted by the Cabinet.

After that midnight meeting, Chamberlain did not relax. Next morning he met Daladier, who admitted that he had not expressed himself well the previous evening, but 'now stated that if Germany attacked Czechoslovakia and hostilities ensued, the French intended to go to war and to commence hostilities with Germany within five days.'[29] This information was confirmed by General Gamelin, speaking on behalf of France's fighting services. Gamelin not only promised an offensive within five days, he also provided some significant information about the current military position: information so secret that it was not circulated with the ordinary Cabinet minutes, although reported to the Cabinet. His appraisal suggested that France was in a position to draw off a significant amount of pressure from Czechoslovakia.

At noon on 26 September the Cabinet met again, and heard the much clearer news from France. They were also regaled with other snippets of information. Churchill had sent a letter, urging that Parliament should be recalled; the Ministers agreed that it should meet in two days' time. Beneš, the Ministers were told, was attempting to buy off Polish threats by an offer to cede Teschen in return for a pact of non-aggression.

There was also some disquietening news from the Dominions. That morning the Colonial Secretary, Malcolm MacDonald, had met the High Commissioners.

> They had all said in the strongest possible terms that, in the view of their Governments, if there was any possible chance of peace by negotiation the opportunity should not be lost. In their view acceptance of Herr Hitler's proposals was better than war. At the same time they had little doubt that if we became involved in war the Dominions would join in too. The Secretary of State added that he thought that while Australia and New Zealand might join us after a short delay, in the case of South Africa and Eire the delay might be rather considerable.

Here indeed was a new complication in the situation. Many days ago, Lord Zetland, Secretary for India, had warned the Cabinet that war against Germany was likely to be the occasion for trouble in India and the Levant; these possible difficulties with the Dominions could prove immensely harmful to morale at home.

There can be little doubt that this consideration disturbed the Cabinet a great deal. Chamberlain played up these anxieties when the Cabinet met in the evening of the following day, Tuesday 27 September. The Dominion High Commissioners 'had all visited Downing Street that afternoon and had all represented that in their view further pressure should be put upon the Czechoslovak Government to accept Herr Hitler's terms.'

If it is suspected that Chamberlain, and perhaps MacDonald, were distorting the views of the self-governing Commonwealth in order to make a point of their own to the Cabinet, the record of that meeting with the Dominion High Commissioners has been preserved, and leaves the reader in no doubt as to the tenor of the discussions.[30] Initiative seems to have sprung from Bruce, of Australia. The South African representative, te Water, went so far as to submit an *aide-mémoire*, asserting categorically that 'South Africa cannot be expected to take any part in a war over Czechoslovakia'.[31] Canadian views do not appear to have been strongly pressed, but the evidence is that they were similar to those of the other Dominions.[32] It was an astonishing and disturbing feature of the situation that whereas domestic opinion[33] and French opinion were becoming increasingly hostile to any settlement which Hitler was likely to accept, yet Dominion opinion was hardening in favour of acceptance of the Godesberg Memorandum. MacDonald still felt the Dominions would join Britain in event of war – 'but it was clear they would come in only halfheartedly and with mental reservations about our policy.'

The news from the Dominions was accompanied by a good deal of further alarming information. Sir Nevile Henderson was reported to be of opinion that, unless Czechoslovakia came to terms with Germany, she would be exposed to the same fate as Abyssinia. The British Military Attaché at Berlin had just visited Czechoslovakia, and received a very poor impression of the morale of the country and the military capacity of its army. When the Prime Minister's emissary, Sir Horace Wilson, saw Hitler, he was assured that there were only two possibilities: either the Czechs would accept his demands, or the Germans would overrun Czechoslovakia – in which case, of course, they would not stop at the ethnic frontier between Czechs and Sudetendeutsch. The Prime Minister gave a further piece of bad news: 'The latest information was that Poland would side with Germany. This would be consistent with the fact that they had rejected the proposals made to them by M. Beneš.'[34]

Neville Chamberlain proposed that, if the Czechs could not bring themselves to accept the modified Godesberg Memorandum, there remained the possibility that they might announce to the world that they were withdrawing troops back to the ethnic frontier, and would not resist the advance of the Germans up to that point. The Prime Minister 'did not propose that we should advise the Czechs to take this course, but merely that we should put this suggestion before them'. The suggestion was set out in a draft telegram to Prague, laid before the Cabinet.

Duff Cooper's response was to declare that 'he could not be associated with' the proposed telegram. Heavier guns were moved into position. Sir John Simon perceived that 'the suggestion . . . amounts to tacit acceptance of Herr Hitler's Memorandum'. Finally, Halifax himself joined the revolt. He 'would feel great difficulty in sending the draft telegram'. Britain had reached an agreement with France a couple of days before, and 'could not depart from those decisions without consulting the French Government'. To do so would be to capitulate to the Germans. He doubted whether the proposal would be accepted by the House of Commons, and furthermore was not convinced that the Germans would stop at the ethnic line.

Chamberlain, faced with an almost universal revolt by his colleagues, backed down. 'The Prime Minister said that the Foreign Secretary had given powerful and perhaps convincing reasons against the adoption of his suggestion. If this was the general view of his colleagues he was prepared to leave it at that.' The telegram was not sent. Finally, the Cabinet wound up its business by ratifying the decision which Chamberlain and Duff Cooper had taken together that afternoon: 'to proceed with the mobilisation of the navy'.

6 Munich

'The tributes that have come in from all over the world are such as no man or woman can ever have received before.'   Neville to Mary Chamberlain, 5 November 1938. NC 1/20/1/186

'I only know that as the hours went by events seemed to be closing in and driving us to the edge of the abyss with a horrifying certainty and rapidity.'[1] Thus wrote the Prime Minister to his sister a few days after the end of the Czechoslovak crisis. In the latter part of September, nearly everything was pointing to war. The Ambassador telegraphed from Paris that there had been a 'complete change' in French opinion; the President of the Chamber assured him that 'an overwhelming majority of the chamber will now be for resistance'.[2] Newton, from Prague, confuted the information received a little earlier about the low morale of the Czechoslovak army; perhaps the frontier guards whom the Berlin Military Attaché had seen were in poor shape, but the ordinary troops showed 'no lack of morale . . . [but] confidence in their arms, their leadership and their equipment.'[3] The Germans, thought the Czech General Staff, would bring against them seventy-five divisions. Though this was more than double the number of which Gamelin had spoken during his visit to London a few days earlier, and also about double the number of Czechs could provide for their own defence, they were not dismayed 'in view of the defence and the interior lines of the German army.'[4]

Meanwhile, diplomats who had once considered that the difference between the Anglo-French proposals and Hitler's Godesberg Memorandum was slight, suddenly began to have second thoughts. British and French Ministers in Prague were shocked to learn that the

> effect of the German memorandum would be to cut Czechoslovakia to pieces and leave her more completely at the mercy of Germany than had been yet realised in either of our legations. Not only would frontier waist north of Brünn be reduced to a width of 60 Km., but all main railway lines connecting Bohemia with Slovakia would pass through territory in German occupation.[5]

From the German side, too, information suggested that the climax was rapidly approaching. The German army was to commence mobilisation at 2 p.m. on Wednesday 28 September. One of the many lessons which men claimed to have learnt from 1914 was that once a major power begins army mobilisation, it is practically impossible to avert war. As for Germany's most important likely ally, Foreign Minister Count Ciano told the British Ambassador that 'Italy's interests, honour and pledged word required that she should side actively and fully with Germany.'[6]

Chamberlain was not the man to abandon his work for peace while any glimmer of hope remained. The letter which he wrote to Hitler on 26 September strongly affirmed the view that negotiations were still possible, and tendered Britain's good offices as mediator to determine the manner and time of transfer of those territories whose allocation to Germany was not in dispute. In the evening of 27 September, some time after the Cabinet meeting, Halifax sent detailed proposals for transfer, which would take place at various dates from 1 to 10 October.

Hitler's reply to Chamberlain was sent later the same evening: he clearly had not seen the detailed proposals. This reply suggested strongly that the Führer's determination to force the issue so urgently sprang from one fundamental cause: his total distrust of the Czechs, and his apprehension that they would always contrive, somehow or other, to procrastinate a final settlement – unless confronted with the actuality or immediate threat of force. The following morning, 28 September, Chamberlain sent a personal message to Hitler:

> After reading your letter I feel certain that you can get all essentials without war and without delay. I am ready to come to Berlin myself at once to discuss arrangements for transfer with you and representatives of Czech Government, together with representatives of France and Italy if you desire. I feel convinced we could reach agreement in a week. However much you distrust Prague Government's intentions, you cannot doubt power of British and French Governments to see that promises are carried out fairly and fully and forthwith. As you know I have stated publicly that we are prepared to undertake that they shall be so carried out.[7]

At lunchtime two telegrams were received from Rome: one indicating that Hitler, at Mussolini's request, had postponed mobilisation until the following day; the other that Mussolini was advising Hitler to accept the proposals for a conference.[8] Everything that happened in the last few days of September indicated that Italy was exceedingly anxious to avert war, and that Mussolini was prepared to exert his influence over Hitler to the uttermost to that effect. The improvement in Anglo-Italian relations since Eden's departure in February gave the Duce a freedom of manoeuvre which he certainly would not have possessed otherwise.

When Chamberlain rose to speak in the House of Commons in the early afternoon of Wednesday 28 September Hitler's reply had not been received, but the news from Italy gave the Prime Minister good reason to be sanguine. While the lengthy and factual record was being given,

Henderson telephoned Sir Alexander Cadogan at the Foreign Office, with information that Hitler had invited Chamberlain, Mussolini and Daladier – no mention of a Czech representative – to meet him at Munich the following day. Chamberlain always had a great sense of dramatic timing; but this particular piece of news timed itself. Sir John Simon, with some difficulty, contrived to attract Chamberlain's attention while the Prime Minister was delivering his speech, and thrust two pieces of paper into his hand. Chamberlain studied them for a considerable time, then reported the tidings to the House of Commons. The scene which followed is described in the *News Chronicle*, whose account is not less impressive when it is recalled that the newspaper had adopted a sharply critical line during the crisis:

> Mr. Chamberlain had to stand silent for nearly five minutes while Members, foreign Ambassadors, press and public jumped to their feet and cheered uproariously. Tears came into the eyes of Queen Mary sitting in the public gallery . . . Generally the 'lobby' feeling was one of profound relief though there are M.P.s in all Parties who fear further German intransigence.[9]

The leaders of the Opposition Parties spoke after Chamberlain. Clement Attlee, for the Labour Party, was

> absolutely sure that everyone in this House would have welcomed the statement of the Prime Minister . . . every member of this House is desirous of neglecting no chance of preserving peace without sacrificing principles. We wish to give the Prime Minister every opportunity of following up this new move.

Sir Archibald Sinclair, for the Liberals, declared

> the feelings of relief which we have felt at the news which he has conveyed in the House . . . He has told us that he is going into this Conference and that he is determined to see that the Czechs carry out the obligations that they have accepted. I hope that he will go with an equal determination to see that the Czechoslovak state in its new frontiers will have a chance of economic survival and complete freedom and independence.

James Maxton, for the I.L.P., concurred; so did George Lansbury, sometime leader of the Labour Party, an old-time socialist with strong pacifist proclivities. The one jarring note in the brief debate was struck by the sole Communist M.P., William Gallacher, who echoed predictably the current Russian view: 'I would not be a party to what has been going on here. There are as many fascists opposite as in Germany, and I protest against the dismemberment of Czechoslovakia.' The Government's most impressive critics – Lloyd George, Churchill, Eden – did not give the House the benefit of their views. No one reading the account of that debate could have any doubt that the House of Commons was practically unanimous in support of Chamberlain's decision to go to Munich.

Nor could any M.P. have had the slightest doubt that a settlement at Munich would necessarily involve transfer of the Sudetenland to Germany. Sinclair actually told them so; and on his return a few days later Chamberlain reminded the House of the situation as it then stood:

> We did not go there to decide whether the predominantly German areas in the Sudetenland should be passed over to the German Reich. That had been decided already. Czechoslovakia had accepted the Anglo-French proposals. What we had to consider was the method, the conditions and the time of the transfer of the territory.

In spite of the altercations which had accompanied the announcement of the Anglo-French plan a week earlier, the Prime Minister was reasonably entitled to assume that if he returned from Munich with a settlement which preserved Czechoslovakia as an independent state, he would have virtually unanimous support from the House of Commons.

Otherwise, why did the M.P.s cheer him? The fears and apprehensions which Attlee and Sinclair expressed were fears that Hitler would turn the screw further, not fears about the wisdom of accepting orderly transfer of the Sudetenland. The proper action for any M.P. who believed that it was wrong to countenance that transfer was to remain in his seat during the demonstration, to urge the Prime Minister to refuse the invitation to Munich, and to tell the House of Commons in so many words that he would prefer war: which, as everyone knew, was the sole possible alternative.

After lunch on Thursday 29 September, Hitler, Chamberlain, Mussolini and Daladier met in conference at Munich, and their discussions continued, with intervals, until 1 a.m. the following day. Chamberlain asked that a representative of Czechoslovakia should also be present, but was assured that the matter was too urgent to permit of the inevitable delay which such a course would involve. The briefness of the Conference suggests that little hard bargaining took place: Hitler was obviously resolved to avoid war provided he could gain the essentials. Chamberlain later told the Cabinet that proceedings would have been briefer still if arrangements had been managed efficiently by the German hosts.

The statesmen assembled at Munich agreed that those parts of Czechoslovakia where there was an undoubted German majority should be evacuated by the Czechs and occupied by the Germans in stages from 1 to 10 October. The detailed procedure of occupation would be decided by an International Commission, which would include representatives of the four major Powers and of Czechoslovakia. The International Commission would also determine the areas where a plebiscite should be held. The plebiscite would be conducted before the end of November under international supervision, following the method which had been applied a few years earlier in the Saar. The International Commission would then propose a definitive frontier, which might deviate slightly from the strict ethnographic line. Individuals who wished to migrate either into or our of the transferred territories were given six months in which to do so. The Czechs would release Sudeten political prisoners, and also would permit any Sudetendeutsch who so desired to resign from the army and the police. By an annex to the agreement, the heads of government agreed to meet again if the question of Hungarian and Polish minorities had not been resolved by agreement within three months. Britain and France guaranteed the new state forthwith; Germany and Italy would do so when the minority questions had been settled. Sir Horace Wilson noted that 'at no time during the Conference did the German representatives raise the question of Czech foreign policy, nor was Russia mentioned.'[10]

After the main business had been concluded, Chamberlain met Hitler without the other Heads of Government present, and asked the Führer to sign a document pledging the two countries to adopt 'the method of consultation' in questions which might arise between them, and undertaking 'to continue our efforts to remove possible sources of difference and thus contribute to assure the peace of Europe.' When the draft was being read to Hitler he repeatedly ejaculated, 'Ja!' Armed not only with the substantive Four-Power agreement but also with the more personal declaration, Chamberlain left Munich later in the morning. Before they departed, Chamberlain and Daladier met the Czech representative, who was 'given a pretty broad hint that – having regard to the seriousness of the alternative – the best course was for his Government to accept what was clearly a considerable improvement upon the Godesberg Memorandum'.[11] Prudently, the Czechs very soon complied.

On Friday 30 September, Chamberlain and Daladier returned to their respective capitals. Each was greeted by wildly enthusiastic crowds. Chamberlain brandished the document he had signed along with Hitler, delivering himself of the opinion that 'peace in our time' had been secured. It is curious that nobody else – not Hitler, not other members of the British Cabinet – seems to have given that particular document much weight.

The same evening the British Cabinet met. In a departure from ordinary procedure, the meeting opened with a fulsome speech from Simon, expressing the Cabinet's admiration for the Prime Minister's efforts.[12] Chamberlain, who 'felt that we could now regard the crisis as ended', first gave a disquisition on the Munich Conference, and then explained how the arrangements differed from those proposed in Hitler's Godesberg Memorandum. In his view,

> The Munich agreement . . . reverted, though not in express terms, to the Anglo-French plan. . . . [It] was a vast improvement, and . . . it represented an orderly way of carrying out the Franco-British proposals. He thought it was a triumph for diplomacy that representatives of the

Four Powers concerned should have met and reached a peaceful settlement of the matter.

Perhaps the most remarkable feature of that Cabinet meeting was the reaction of Duff Cooper to the Prime Minister's statement. Throughout the crisis, he had been the most intransigent opponent of Chamberlain's policy within the Government. He obviously could not resign while the issue of peace or war was in doubt; but he admitted that he had come to the post-Munich meeting of the Cabinet prepared to do so. He still 'felt a considerable uneasiness in regard to the position', and would need to discuss it further with the Prime Minister; yet he confessed to his colleagues that 'after the detailed explanation given by the Prime Minister, he recognised that the differences between the Godesberg Memorandum and the Munich agreement were much greater than he had previously recognised.'

Initial reactions when the terms of Munich were known were far from hostile to Chamberlain. Only the Communist *Daily Worker* – faithful as ever to the current Russian view – was bitter: 'Neville Chamberlain returned smiling to Britain yesterday from the greatest betrayal of the century.'[13] The very moderate comments of Labour's *Daily Herald* were far more typical of the responsible Opposition: 'Summing up we must say that this plan is open to grave criticism on a number of points. Nevertheless Herr Hitler has had to abandon the most brutal of his Godesberg terms.'[14] The often critical *Daily Telegraph* had no reservations: 'The news will be hailed with a profound and universal relief.'[15]

It is easy enough to make the mistake of identifying 'public opinion' with the opinion of the press, the politicians, or even of the more demonstrative members of the nation at large. All of these vociferous folk together form but a tiny minority of the British nation. It rather looks as if the people who sent letters to Opposition M.P.s and Opposition newspapers were, for the most part, bitterly critical. If so, this may well have influenced politicians who were personally in doubt. Certainly there was a far more hostile reaction in Parliament in the four-day debate which commenced on Monday 3 October than the noisy demonstrations which accompanied Chamberlain's departure and return, or the early comments of the press, had given reason to expect.

The Parliamentary discussion ranged across both the immediate crisis and the foreign policy of the Government over a long period. Duff Cooper had decided to persist in his contemplated resignation, and the Personal Statement which he made was an important contribution to the debate. Cooper was in a somewhat difficult position, for – as he admitted to the House – he was implicated in the Cabinet decision to urge cession of the Sudetenland. This position he defended on the grounds that 'if we were obliged to go to war it would be hard to have it said against us that we were fighting against the principle of self-determination'. The nub of the former

First Lord's attack was that the Government had failed to make its own position clear to the dictators – men who did not understand diplomatic subtleties, but rather 'the language of the mailed fist'. Sir Samuel Hoare, Home Secretary, met Cooper on these grounds: 'If we had made an ultimatum in the days immediately before the Nuremberg speech Europe would today have been plunged into a world war.'

Cooper's resignation was inevitably hailed by the Opposition with glee similar to that with which they had received Eden's resignation in February. It is striking to recall, however, that on the earlier occasion Cooper had strongly supported Chamberlain in the Cabinet, and afterwards continued stressing the need 'to think of Italy as a potential ally'.[16] Conservative rebels were by no means all men with similar approaches to diplomatic questions.

Just as Cooper could only criticise the Government on a narrow front because he shared responsibility for its most controversial decision, so also in the circumstances of the debate the Government could hardly provide its most compelling answer. They had not given a firm commitment to the Czechs during the previous six months largely because they feared such commitment would encourage the Czechs to resist even reasonable claims from the Sudetendeutsch, and would further encourage the French bluff. In the crisis they avoided a challenge partly because the moral issue and likely world reactions were far from certain; partly because the military evidence suggested that if war must come, delay would be to Britain's advantage; partly because there was some scintilla of possibility that Hitler might keep his word. No Minister could say those things to the House of Commons and the world; and because it could not be stated at the time, the Government's case has largely gone by default ever since.

Throughout the debate, critics of the Government seem to have had considerable difficulty in deciding where the weight of their attack should fall. Hugh Dalton, for the Labour Party, criticised the odd diplomatic arrangements which prevailed during the crisis, and went on to argue that 'the Prime Minister was unduly hustled, intimidated and outmanoeuvered by Herr Hitler in these conversations'. Sir Archibald Sinclair, for the Liberals, recorded his 'foreboding that we shall yet live to rue the day when His Majesty's Government sold the pass of freedom in Central Europe.'

Far the most impressive critic on the Government side was Churchill:

I will therefore begin by saying the most unpopular and most unwelcome thing. I will begin by saying what everybody would like to ignore or forget, but which must nevertheless be stated, namely that we have sustained a total and unmitigated defeat, and that France has suffered even more than we have.

He returned to the point he had made in March: that Britain should have declared straight out and a long time beforehand that she would, with others, join to protect Czechoslovakia against unprovoked aggression. His Majesty's Government refused to give the guarantee when it would have saved the situation, yet in the end they gave it when it was too late, and now, for the future, they renew it when they have not the slightest power to make it good.

The Conservative critics of the Government are now famous; the men in the Opposition Parties who spoke in its support are less so. James Maxton, for the I.L.P., recalled how his own small Party had 'made, more than a week ago, an unequivocal statement that if war took place, we should be in opposition to that war'. Just as Churchill spoke uncomfortable home truths on one side, so did Maxton on the other: 'The Prime Minister did something that the mass of the common people in the world wanted done'. One Labour M.P., James Barr, told the House that his own response to Munich was to send Chamberlain a two-word telegram: 'Heartiest congratulations'.

Other noted members of Opposition Parties who did not sit in the House of Commons wrote to Chamberlain to similar effect. Ben Tillett, the veteran Trade Unionist, wrote of the Prime Minister's 'nobility in . . . endeavour', adding: 'Some day the wonderful part you have played with patience to avert the degradation and brutality, will be estimated for its worth and meaning.'[17] Chamberlain had Liberal admirers, too. Not least significant of these was Viscount Samuel – former Cabinet Minister, sometime Leader of the Liberal M.P.s and perhaps the most distinguished British Jew of his time:

> I would offer you my warmest congratulations. I have followed the course of the negotiations, not only with full sympathy for the object in view but with complete agreement with the course you have taken at every stage. Any fool can go to war, but it often needs the highest qualities of statesmanship to keep the peace. These you have shown in full measure . . .[18]

The division which followed that debate was, predictably, governed by three-line whips operated by the Parties. In the view of one of the Conservative critics, Harold Macmillan, there were further pressures at work. There was a move by some members of the Government for an immediate General Election – 'thinking that Chamberlain, as Saviour of Peace, will sweep the country'. There was also a belief that Conservative rebels would be 'marked down for destruction and official Tory candidates run against them'.[19] Towards the end of the debate, Chamberlain made it quite clear that the Government had no intention of calling an early General Election designed to cash in on his popularity. Such an election would have set Chamberlain's foreign policy at unnecessary risk, and would have inflamed political feelings at the very moment when he desired them to abate.

In the event, the Government won its majority of over two hundred. No Conservative voted against the Government and no Labour M.P. in favour. It is difficult to be sure how many on either side deliberately abstained and how many were paired or absent for good cause. It appears that twenty – perhaps thirty – Conservatives abstained deliberately: a very impressive band, including Churchill, Eden, Duff Cooper, Harold Macmillan, L. S. Amery and Brenden Bracken. A junior Minister, Captain Crookshank, got to the point of drafting a resignation speech on grounds similar to those of Cooper,[20] but finally remained in the Government and voted with it. Apparently about eighteen Labour M.P.s did not vote;[21] The I.L.P. formally abstained. The Liberals, who had less power than the great Parties to discipline their rebels, were significantly split: fourteen supported the official anti-Government line, four voted in Chamberlain's support.

In the immediate aftermath of the debate, no Party was without its troubles. The many important Conservative abstentions could not fail to disquieten Government supporters in the country. A former Labour M.P., Hector Hughes, resigned rather noisily from his Party because he agreed with Chamberlain. Viscount Samuel made his disagreement with Sinclair as unobtrusive as possible, but one Liberal M.P., Herbert Holdsworth, crossed to the Government side of the House. Even Maxton found himself under fire from some members of his little band of I.L.P.-men.[22]

As the September crisis receded into the past, men began to take measure of what had happened, in more reflective vein. The period had been characterised by the most astonishing diplomatic improvisations. Ostensibly, the quarrel lay originally between the Czechoslovak Government and the Sudetendeutsch, later between the Czechoslovak Government and the Reich. More realistically, it seemed to lie between France, as Czechoslovakia's guarantor, and Germany. Yet at no point in the acute phase of the crisis did France make the running on the Allied side: always it was Britain who did so.

More remarkable still was the way in which ordinary channels of diplomatic contact were circumvented. If the British Government wished to discuss matters of mutual concern with France, then the French Ministers were summoned to London: nobody thought of settling the question between Halifax and Corbin, or between Bonnet and Phipps. Between Britain and Germany, communications were even more unorthodox. It was the Prime Minister, not the Foreign Secretary, who conducted the negotiations on Britain's side; Hitler and not Ribbentrop on the side of Germany. As Duff Cooper pointed out in the House of Commons, the German Ambassador was not in London from start to finish of the crisis; the German Chargé d'Affaires rarely visited the Foreign Office. Henderson was never regarded as the leading British negotiator, although there is some evidence that he exerted a considerable, perhaps a decisive, effect upon Göring. Henderson in any case was a sick man, and soon after the crisis needed to return to Britain for a major operation.

Permanent officials were even more completely by-passed. Cadogan was on leave for the latter part of August and the beginning of September; nobody seems to have missed him. Dalton reminded the House of Commons in the post-Munich debate that neither Vansittart nor Cadogan accompanied Chamberlain on his German visits. Foreign Office officials of the other Powers also slid into the background: even Léger was inconspicuous, while the German State Secretary, Weizsäcker, was totally insignificant.

Chamberlain and Hitler obviously dominated the two sides; but it is well to remember that neither got his way completely. Chamberlain had favoured acceptance of the Godesberg Memorandum, but was overruled by his colleagues; no doubt the Prime Minister was later very glad that this had happened. Hitler is usually seen as the man who carried everything before him; but in fact he did not. There can be little doubt that he hoped to obtain not merely control of the Sudetenland but the total collapse of Czechoslovakia in the autumn of 1938. Perhaps he had other objects, too; but these will need discussion later.

One of the innumerable rumours which sprang out of the Munich meeting told that Hitler and Mussolini met before the main conference. Mussolini, the story goes, saluted Hitler with words to the effect that there must be no war. Hitler vigorously asserted the contrary, and the two men retired to a railway carriage, where they proceeded to shout at each other for two hours.[23] Another tale tells that Hitler was very 'abnormal' at the main conference, sitting with his back to the other delegates 'making grimaces and biting his nails'[24] These, surely, are symptoms of frustration. Another extraordinary rumour – categorically denied elsewhere – told that the Germans plied Daladier with so much liquor at lunchtime that he was in no condition to contribute much to the discussions: 'He only focussed when the final terms were being read out. He then rose and began a long, indignant speech, declaring that the terms were impossible, but then went out of action again.'[25]

As with the speeches which Greek and Roman authors put into the mouths of their historical figures, we do not need to believe that these incidents actually occurred to accept that they possess some symbolic meaning. Hitler may very well have been banking on Mussolini's assistance, and then discovered that the Duce would not, or could not, give him the help anticipated. Drunk or sober, Daladier really had nothing to say at Munich which Chamberlain could not have said on his behalf.

What was never set to the test was the strength and resolution of the Soviet Union. She had affirmed repeatedly her determination to stand by Czechoslovakia if France did so as well. Beneš' story that the Soviet Union at one point promised unilateral assistance was known in Britain at least by the spring of 1940.[26] Undoubtedly Soviet diplomats and apologists abroad exploited the propaganda content of the story to the limit. Maisky, for example, poured complaints into the ears of British Opposition politicians like Lloyd George and Dalton,[27] arguing that the Soviet Union had been willing and anxious to help Czechoslovakia, but had been cold-shouldered by the British and French Governments. There were many people in the West, by no means all Communists or Communist sympathisers, to whom such arguments made powerful appeal. They were not always eager to quantify the assistance which the Soviet Union would have rendered; or to analyse the consequences which would have supervened if she had rendered all the assistance of which they believed her capable: by sending, for example, the Red Army across the frontiers of a resentful Poland.

One thing alone was certain. Munich was not, could not be, an 'end'. Even if one credited Hitler's repeated assertion that he had no further territorial aims in Europe, he assuredly had economic and diplomatic aims in Europe, and territorial aims elsewhere, which would require attention. The Parliamentary and national debate on Munich had been intensely charged with emotion on both sides; relief at escape from a seemingly inevitable war on one side; shame and anger on the other. Both kinds of emotion would soon evaporate. Those who had felt relief would begin to count the cost; those who had felt anger would begin to prepare for another encounter.

7 Aftermath

'If M. Bonnet is our strongest rampart against Hitler, then indeed I feel inclined to despair.'   Duff Cooper to Sir Eric Phipps, 7 December 1938. PHPP 3/2 fo. 30

'With cholera on the right and bubonic plague on the left I prefer to steer a middle course with any other state ready to do likewise.'
Phipps to Cooper, 8 December 1938 (copy). PHPP 3/2 fo. 31

Neville Chamberlain's first major political task after Munich was to remodel the Cabinet. Apparently the pressure for including some of the Government's critics was quite strong, but he beat it down. It would hardly augur well for appeasement if men were incorporated into the Ministry who had proclaimed to the world their belief that Hitler was a monster who could only be restrained by force or the threat of force. It was necessary to replace Duff Cooper; and an unexpected vacancy was created by the death of the Dominions Secretary, Lord Stanley – brother of Oliver Stanley. Furthermore, the Prime Minister was less than ecstatic about the calibre of those who remained: 'It is necessary to get extra strength and I cannot see it among any of the younger men.'[1]

Chamberlain was much impressed by Runciman's work, and wished to bring him back into the Cabinet.[2] Runciman did not feel equal to the strain of a Department, and his views about the general calibre of his proposed colleagues were similar to those of the Prime Minister.[3] In order to make room for Runciman, Chamberlain needed to displace the Lord President of the Council, Viscount Hailsham – a decision which he regretted on personal, but not on public, grounds: 'he is one of my oldest political friends and, as so often happens, does not realise that he is no longer able to do his work'.[4] There was a further complication, for at that moment Hailsham's son, Quintin Hogg, was defending Oxford for the Government in a critical by-election. Accordingly the announcement was postponed until the contest was safely out of the way.

A more startling Cabinet appointment was also considered: Viscount Samuel. Chamberlain's motives included calculations of public good and political craft: 'He has very considerable ability and his appointment would broaden the basis and – be a nasty smack for Master Archie. I have been interested to find that the idea appeals to my Chief Whip.'[5] The post suggested was another non-departmental office: Lord Privy Seal. Samuel was completely astonished at the approach, and much torn between conflicting considerations. Runciman's impending return was an obvious incentive, for the two men were old friends and political colleagues, though latterly opponents. More important was Samuel's approval of the Munich policy, and his feeling that this carried some obligation to assist its further implementation. On the other hand he was at variance with the Government over the proposed pact with Italy, and particularly conscious of obligations to his Liberal colleagues. For them, a decision to join the Government would be 'a great shock and . . . deeply resented'.[6] Samuel consulted only his wife, and the Marquess of Crewe, Liberal leader in the Lords. Crewe's first response was a delightfully cryptic telegram: 'Must not altogether discourage investment but see much difficulty in limited liability'. This was followed by an explanatory letter, in which Crewe argued that Samuel would become implicated in the general policies of the Government, and would come to occupy a position which the public could hardly distinguish from that of Simon or Runciman:[7] both of whom Liberals generally regarded as apostates. Reluctantly, but with a strong sense of loyalty to his Party colleagues, Samuel declined the offer. Accordingly, the Cabinet changes announced towards the end of October were a good deal less dramatic than they might have been. The only member of the old Cabinet who was dropped was Hailsham; the only men who entered were Runciman and Sir John Anderson – the latter being better known as an administrator than as a politician.

The overwhelming question which confronted Britain and the world was whether the Munich settlement could become the foundation of a new international order, based on reconciliation between the Powers. Probably this notion, on which Chamberlain in particular had set his heart, never really had a chance. Reconciliation presupposed not merely the mutual interest of the Powers in averting war and reducing the universal burden of armaments; it also depended on genuine goodwill and trust in all major countries. This palpably did not exist. The British people – whether or not they regarded Munich as preferable to war – did not think of it as a just and equable settlement. A man may hand over his watch at pistol point; no power on earth can prevent him feeling resentment at the transaction, or yearning for the day when the robber shall be brought to justice. The bitter, outraged patriotism of Conservatives like Churchill and Labour men like George Dallas is familiar enough. So also is the anguished idealism of a great section of the Labour and Liberal Parties, and of Conservatives in the tradition of Viscount Cecil, to whom Nazism was not merely an international danger but a moral abomination.

Even the men who counselled the Munich settlement on the British side, really resented it. While the issue of peace or war still hung in the balance, Sir Nevile Henderson – putative pro-German – prefaced his recommendation that the Sudetenland should be ceded to Hitler with the angry words, 'Hateful though it is to give in to these wolves . . .'[8] *The Times*, for all its dangerous advocacy of a Sudeten *Anschluss*, was drawing its own moral some days before Munich: that Britain should derive 'plain warning that we must tackle the question of our defences more seriously than in the past.'[9] In the immediate aftermath of the settlement, the message that Britain must look to her armaments was drawn in a more uninhibited manner. On 7 October, the day after the great Munich debate, the *Daily Express* – which had supported Chamberlain – came out in favour of compulsory military service in terms which delighted an anti-Munich Conservative like L. S. Amery.[10] Sir Alexander Cadogan, whom nobody in the world could accuse of fire-eating, was keenly conscious of the problems which affected his own Department: 'In our (and France's) present condition of dangerous inferiority to Germany in military strength it is difficult to have or to pursue a foreign policy. Therefore our first need is to get on more equal terms.'[11]

Thus the moral that Britain must greatly accelerate her rearmament was generally taken in official and pro-Government circles. Six weeks on from Munich, Hankey assessed the views of his own many influential contacts on the role which the Prime Minister would play:

> The truth is that Chamberlain, while at the Treasury, absorbed many of the ideas of that Department. He will give freely to the Navy and Air Force, but he is very niggardly, I think, to the Army . . . Though we may not get the best value for our money, we shall get a good navy and air force, which is our primary need, and that will satisfy most people . . . But if France needs an army to help her – as she will – we shall be no better than in 1914, in fact worse . . .'[12]

The first Cabinet meeting which gave detailed attention to defence after Munich was on 7 November. The euphoria had not yet evaporated; both Chamberlain and Halifax were anxious to avoid any measures which might vitiate further *détente* with Germany. Yet increases in armaments whose purpose was in the narrowest sense of the term 'defensive' could scarcely endanger international understanding. Nobody, for example, could cavil at proposals for a substantial increase in anti-aircraft guns, and it was easy to persuade the Cabinet to accept proposals which were set before it. Chamberlain was 'not altogether happy' at the Admiralty request for twenty new escort vessels, but nevertheless led his colleagues to accept the recommendation, subject to possible reconsideration later.[13]

Far more difficult was the question of air rearmament. Sir Kingsley Wood had circulated a lengthy document to his colleagues, which analysed the position at considerable depth.[14] 'Had we now been at war,' wrote the Air Minister,

> the intensity of our efforts in the air would have very rapidly declined as our aircraft and their crews became casualties; it would, on the most optimistic estimate, have been very many months before our production

of aircraft and war training of crews could have enabled us to resume the minimum essential rate of war effort.

It was one thing, however, to say that aircraft production was inadequate; a much more difficult matter to decide how and where it should be improved. This was particularly hard when it became necessary to decide between the claims of fighters and bombers. When General Ismay made his assessment in September, he drew an important comparison: 'In land warfare the defence enjoys a preponderating advantage over the attack. In the air, on the other hand, the balance of advantage at present rests decidedly with the attacker.'[15] With such opinions doubtless in mind, Sir Kingsley Wood argued in Cabinet in favour of a heavy bomber programme as 'the best means of enabling this country to get on level terms with Germany'.[16] The military case for bombers perhaps showed itself later to be less strong than appeared in 1938. In any event, it was countered by two arguments. Fighters were weapons of defence in the narrow sense of the word, while bombers were weapons of attack, and thus provocative to Germany and inimical to an 'Appeasement' policy. Furthermore, a bomber cost about four times as much as a fighter. Both Chamberlain and Simon argued that the cost of a major bomber programme would set severe strains on the economy. The Cabinet eventually resolved to accept a 30 per cent increase in fighters, at a cost of £45 millions, but only to place bomber orders in sufficient quantities to keep the factories in full production. Questions relating to army expansion were not considered in Cabinet at any depth at that stage, although they cropped up from time to time in other discussions, and would eventually pose some very difficult political and international problems.

The possible reorientation of British Foreign Policy in light of the September crisis came under consideration among diplomatic officials, although their views did not crystallise quickly enough to enable any concrete proposals to be set before the Cabinet. The general drift of their ideas, however, became fairly clear in the month after Munich. Ashton-Gwatkin, who returned to the Foreign Office after the collapse of the Runciman Mission, wrote: 'The German victory over Czechoslovakia is probably one of the decisive events of history. In one blow it has broken the French system of continental alliances . . . and the advance guard of Soviet Russia in Central Europe.'[17] Cadogan, whose analysis was similar, tried to derive morals for the future. After emphasising the need for rearmament he continued 'We must try to maintain our influence in Western Europe and the Mediterranean. We must cut our losses in Central and Eastern Europe – let Germany, if she can, find there her Lebensraum, and establish herself, if she can, as a powerful economic unit.'[18] Halifax himself at first seemed to accept this general reasoning.[19] The logical conclusion would evidently be for Britain to set pressure upon France – if, indeed, pressure were needed – to 'disinterest' herself from Eastern

Europe. Long before any final decisions could be taken on that question, however, some important events had taken place within the Reich, which radically affected the whole climate of British official opinion.

Germany, like Britain, took some time in assessing the events of September and their implications for the future. A few weeks after Munich, Sir Samuel Hoare sent Chamberlain a memorandum from William Astor, who had just visited Germany. Astor was a Conservative M.P., and a leading figure in the ill-defined social-cum-political 'Cliveden set' – which was widely considered in Opposition circles to exert a great and pernicious effect upon Government policy. Hoare conveyed Astor's observations with the note, 'His conclusions seem to me not be worth attention'. Astor reported that the atmosphere in Berlin was one of relief that peace had been preserved, not one of rejoicing at a bloodless victory. Yet to this statement he made a significant qualification: 'This is the view of the upper classes, middle classes and some of the army and the older members of the working class. On the other hand the young people and the masses of the working class were and are behind Hitler . . . Indeed, what strikes one in Germany is how very socialistic it is . . .'[20] Astor went on to declare that some of the German leaders had wanted a small war against Czechoslovakia; instead, Britain faced Hitler with 'two alternatives: a world war or gaining his point peacefully . . . as there were many forces in Germany against a world war he accepted the peaceful solution, but not gratefully.' The 'small war' would have proved German power to other states, and made them willing to compound on adverse terms.

It is easy to dismiss Astor's memorandum as a specimen of the tittle-tattle with which diplomatic literature of the period is gorged full; but much both of previous and of subsequent history seems to fit in with the view that it was not far from the truth.

At one point in September, Hitler had seemed willing to go to war to enforce his 'Godesberg' proposals, yet at Munich he settled on the 'Berchtesgaden' terms. What made him retreat? Perhaps he had been bluffing and his bluff was called; or perhaps his military advisers suddenly confronted him with new evidence which made him draw back. There were other possible explanations. He may have discovered that Mussolini would not back him. Astor's memorandum suggests that a large number of Germans viewed the prospect of war with horror; and he went on to say that on one important public occasion in the crisis Hitler was greeted by silence and some hisses in Berlin. Another possibility was that he perceived advantages from a durable settlement with Britain and France which would bring him international 'respectability'.

The German press in the immediate aftermath of Munich provides oblique evidence of a great power-struggle within the Nazi Party itself, between those who desired reconciliation with Britain in the spirit of Munich, and those who sought further confrontations with Britain. On 12 October the *Deutsche Allgemeine Zeitung* complained of the 'regular rearmament propaganda campaign' in Britain, singling out two members of the Cabinet – Earl Winterton and Sir Kingsley Wood – for special attack. Next day the whole German press took up the cue; yet the following day the campaign was suddenly dropped.[21] For a considerable time the German press blew hot and cold on the question of British rearmament, sometimes asserting that the arms proposed were much in excess of defensive needs and were pointed against Germany; sometimes declaring that any nation had the right to choose its own level of armaments. While Henderson was away ill in London, Sir George Ogilvie-Forbes acted as Chargé d'Affaires in Berlin; in his view 'the whole matter seems to be one on which the Ministry of propaganda has not yet fully made up its mind'.[22] All this seems to fit more closely with the 'power struggle' explanation than with any other.

The 'radical' Nazis who desired confrontation could easily play on whatever action the Western Democracies might choose to take. If Britain and France were pacific, this was proof that they were weak and irresolute: that the present was the ideal moment to avenge past injuries and secure the future for Germany. If the Western countries were truculent, this was proof that they were plotting hostile action against the Reich, and emphasised the need to forestall them. Above all the 'radical' Nazis could play on the Führer's personal sensitivity. Many people in Britain, including a number of politicians, made no secret of their feelings – the implacable hatred they felt towards the Nazi leaders personally as well as politically. Whether such critics carried many guns in Britain hardly mattered: their undiplomatic utterances could readily be retailed to Hitler. There is no doubt that he resented deeply the philippics launched against him in the post-Munich debate – complaining to the French Ambassador in Berlin that he had been 'insulted' in the House of Commons.[23]

The event which led to the victory of the 'radical' Nazis who sought confrontation took place in Paris on 7 November. A German diplomat was shot and fatally wounded by a young Polish Jew. Next evening, The Times's Berlin correspondent wrote that the 400,000 Jews who remained in Germany were in imminent fear of 'another attack upon their race which . . . will exceed in violence and thoroughness any Jewish "purge" that has taken place during the past five years.'

At 2 a.m. on 10 November the storm broke. An obviously systematic pogrom took place all over the Reich. Thirty-five or forty thousand Jews were arrested; 166 synagogues destroyed; in Berlin alone, 3000 shops were wrecked – whence the name, *Kristallnacht*, by which the occasion became known. To see the situation in perspective, however, it is noteworthy that even *Kristallnacht* apparently did not witness actual murders of Jews.[24] Germany was still a long way from the horrors of the 'final solution', but was moving rapidly in that direction.

No doubt various considerations contributed to these events. To the actual participants, simple greed for plunder was probably a motive; conjoined, perhaps, with crude hatred. For the Nazi leaders who encouraged the crime, there may have been a larger design of plunder: to drive Jews from Germany in precipitate haste, so that they should leave their property behind. It is possible, as Henderson later suggested, that another consideration was to set all Jews in fear of committing political assassination, lest awful revenge be wreaked not only on the individual concerned but also upon his whole people. One may guess that the 'radical' Nazis encouraged *Kristallnacht* in order to polarise opinion and wreck any chance of international goodwill. Whether this was the intention or not, it was certainly the effect of *Kristallnacht*. The incident sent a wave of revulsion through Britain which made any further 'Appeasement' impossible, at least for a very long time. Chamberlain may have caught some glimpse of Hitler's mind; he certainly did not understand the minds of the revolutionary plotters who engineered *Kristallnacht*, whose overriding concern was to produce confrontations, both at home and abroad. A few days after the event, he wrote with evident mystification:

> I am horrified by the Germans' behaviour to the Jews. There does seem to be some fatality about Anglo-German relations which invariably blocks every effort to improve them. I suppose I shall have to say something on the subject tomorrow . . . It will be [a] problem how to avoid condonation on one side or on the other such criticisms as may bring even more things on the heads of these unhappy victims.[25]

Halifax drew, almost casually, the baleful conclusion which he delivered to the Cabinet Committee on Foreign Policy: 'In present circumstances no useful purpose would be served by a resumption at the present time of the contemplated Anglo-German negotiations.'[26] 'Appeasement' of Germany, if not dead, was certainly in a state of suspended animation. The 'radical' Nazis had won the first round. From now on, feelings of mutual antagonism in Germany and the Western Democracies could be expected to escalate; and there were plenty of people on both sides who would gleefully speed the process.

What of Britain's ally, France? In the period immediately after Munich, many people in Czechoslovakia and a few people in Britain viewed her part in the proceedings with massive resentment. The most extreme British opinion was that of General Spears – once a Lloyd George Liberal, currently a Conservative M.P., and close associate of Churchill. Spears 'considered France to have been so completely disgraced that no right-thinking Englishman should shake a Frenchman's hand'.[27] In general, however, there seems to have been a substantial measure of mutual sympathy between the two countries. The Russians were angry at both; but when – just after Munich – Litvinov upbraided Bonnet for France's part in the proceedings, the Frenchman's reply was pointed though gentle: 'The three countries that Russia objected to – viz.,

Germany, Italy and Franco Spain, all happened to be neighbours of France. If they were in South America it might be less necessary to get on decent terms with them.'[28] A day or two later Hankey, who had recently retired from his post with the Cabinet and become a Suez Canal Director, reported the 'intense relief and gratitude to the British Government in general and the Prime Minister in particular'[29] felt by his French colleagues on the Board. That reaction was perhaps not surprising in such quarters; but it appears to have represented the general view of the French nation. The post-Munich debate in Britain had revealed a profound split of opinion, not least in the Conservative Party; a similar challenge to Daladier in the French Chamber produced overwhelming support for the Government's policy: 535 deputies supporting the Prime Minister, only 75 voting against. All but two of the seventy-five were Communists.

In such circumstances, Chamberlain might expect great demonstrations of good will if he chose to visit France; but there were also matters of substance which required consideration. Each country was far from happy about the other's preparedness for war. France's air force was particularly weak, and the British were not convinced that French aircraft production had yet been inaugurated on a satisfactory scale. The French considered that Britain's contribution on land to the common cause would be fatuously small; and some French military men were anxious that Britain should exert pressure on the French Government to improve their country's defences.[30] Through British initiative, an invitation to Paris was secured for Chamberlain and Halifax, along with their wives, late in November. The ostensibly social character of the occasion would leave only a few hours for serious discussions, and an enormous number of matters required to be raised. Some Foreign Office officials felt anxiety about other matters than France's military effectiveness. Sir Orme Sargent warned of 'the almost universal pacifist sentiment in France' and expressed apprehensions about the whole system of French guarantees – including even her alliance with Britain.[31] Another official noted that the German Government had been a good deal more friendly towards France than towards Britain, with evident desire to separate the two countries. He went on to add that 'M. Daladier and M. Bonnet, who were both weak men, might be tempted further along the path of *rapprochement* with Germany than was desirable.'[32]

The meeting between the Ministers took place on 24 November. As often happens on important occasions, the strongest apprehensions which had been felt beforehand were largely allayed, but difficulties were encountered on a different question.[33] There was plain speaking about military preparedness on both sides, but both appear to have been somewhat reassured. Foreign Office fears that France might be prised apart from her British alliance proved groundless. The matter which proved most intractable was the form of the British guarantee to Czechoslovakia. To that we shall return later; suffice for the moment to say that a useful formula was agreed which removed the danger of serious dissension between the Western Democracies.

The effect of the Paris visit was soon obliterated by two other events in the same city. Early in December Ribbentrop paid a visit, and a Franco-German declaration was signed. This 'somewhat anodyne' document had little effect on the policy of either country, but it did provide renewed warning that relations between them might improve at Britain's expense. In contrast with this demonstration of goodwill towards France, the German press engaged in 'continued venomous attacks' on Britain, and Chamberlain sadly noted 'the failure of Hitler to make the slightest gesture of friendliness.'[34] Whether by accident or design, Ribbentrop's visit to Paris coincided with a speech made there by Duff Cooper, who vigorously attacked the Munich policy. Phipps attempted, with a measure of success, to tone down its contents – although, in Chamberlain's view, 'what was left seems to have been mischievous and untimely enough.'[35] Duff Cooper's speech was significant because it was likely to appeal to elements of the French right and centre, who had hitherto supported the Munich policy.

Relations between Britain and the fourth 'Munich Power' also came under active consideration. Agreement between Britain and Italy had been reached in outline as far back as May, but had not yet been brought into force. In the summer, no doubt, preoccupation with the Czech crisis swept everything else aside; but there remained another serious difficulty. The French were always fearful that Mussolini sought a Franco victory in Spain not merely in order to set up a régime with an ideology similar to his own, but also to establish Italian bases which could be used against France in a Mediterranean war. This fear and anxiety about Italy survived the change of government in France which took place in the spring, with its accompanying shift to the right. As in so many other matters of the late 1930s, military considerations took priority over political.

When the Anglo-Italian agreement was finally signed, on 16 November, Lord Perth took the occasion to raise with Count Ciano a suggestion which Mussolini had broached at Munich: that Chamberlain should soon visit Rome. The idea was taken up by Mussolini with some alacrity, and an invitation speedily issued to Chamberlain and Halifax.[36]

Yet while Germany was evidently trying to play off France against Britain by combining friendly approaches to the former with increased hostility towards the latter, Italy suddenly showed signs of attempting to drive a wedge between the Western Democracies from the opposite side. At the very end of November, a noisy demonstration took place in the Italian Chamber. Delegates shouted 'Tunisia!' and this was taken up by visitors in the public gallery who shouted references to Corsica, Nice and Jibuti – all of them places where French and Italian interests were in conflict.[37]

Chamberlain's first reaction was of bewilderment. 'What fools the dictators are!' he wrote to his sister a few days later; 'After the Jews in

Germany, the Italians go and work up this ridiculous demonstration against France, which can only have the effect of uniting all France against them and encouraging all enemies of the Fascist state in their country.'[38] The Prime Minister, whose anger often tended to become stronger rather than weaker as he took full measure of past events, soon began to feel sympathy with the *Daily Herald's* plea that he should cancel the projected Rome visit,[39] and his concern went far beyond those rather self-pitying letters to his sisters. Cadogan wrote to Perth, expressing doubts about the value of the visit; but the Ambassador reacted with horror: 'If the visit were now cancelled the effect would be disastrous for Anglo-Italian relations, and I should regard the future with something akin to despair.'[40] The substance of Chamberlain's view, however, was duly communicated to Ciano by the Ambassador, and anti-French propaganda in Italy speedily declined.

After that, there were no further alarms to vitiate the prospect of the Italian visit. Chamberlain himself felt considerable apprehensions,[41] and the Chiefs of Staff were anxious that no agreement should emerge which might involve concessions in defence of the Mediterranean; but the actual encounter proved a good deal less difficult than the Prime Minister had been disposed to fear. The visit was not marked by any significant decisions: ' "mixing" seems to have been the catchword', wrote Sir Thomas Inskip in his diary.[42] Chamberlain's impressions of Mussolini – whom he found 'straightforward and considerate' – were substantially more favourable than those he had formed of Hitler. 'Halifax', wrote Chamberlain, 'who went expecting not to like him came away with a very favourable impression.'[43] An interesting, and perhaps unfamiliar, side of Mussolini's character was also observed: 'He, the Duce, had always used his influence with Franco on the side of humanity to prisoners and civilians. He had repeatedly sent him letters and telegrams and he considered that he had saved the lives of 50,000 people in Bilbao of whom otherwise very few might have escaped.'[44]

Thus stood relations between the four Great Powers of Europe, three and a half months after Munich. The two alliances had each rather strengthened in the interim, despite half-hearted attempts by Germany to suborn France and by Britain and Italy to suborn each other: but the prospect of any permanent understanding between the four 'Munich Powers' had diminished substantially. At the beginning of December the New Zealand High Commissioner had taxed Malcolm MacDonald with a very loaded question. Ever since Munich, suggested the Dominion representative, 'the assumption had seemed to be that war was inevitable and that it was necessary to increase armaments at once. Was the agreement signed by the Prime Minister valueless?'[45] No real answer could possibly be given to such a question; but when the old issue of the former German colonies was raised, the Dominions Secretary came as close as he could to a reply: 'The atmosphere had indeed completely changed in the past few months and public opinion had hardened to an extraordinary degree. After the attacks on the Jews in Germany it was impossible for either the United Kingdom or the French Government to propose to their Parliaments to hand over natives to German rule.' Even the South African, te Water, 'agreed with the Secretary of State's estimate of public opinion on the subject. Public opinion had also changed elsewhere and he knew, for example, that Mr. Pirow had changed his own views.' Pirow, South African Minister for Defence, had just returned from a visit to various European countries; and during that visit Germany and Italy had been at particular pains to make him feel welcome.

In Britain for certain, and probably in the other 'Munich Powers' as well, events had acquired a momentum of their own which nobody could stop, even though the drift to war was quite contrary to the intentions of at least three of the Heads of Government who met at Munich.

8 Popular Front

'Like so many orators, Cripps believes in the illusory magic of great
public meetings, without comprehending in' the slightest that a
movement does not evolve by spontaneous combustion; an adequate and
competent organisation to cash-in on the enthusiasm engendered by the
meeting is a pre-requisite.'   T. F. Tweed to Lloyd George, 16 March
1939. L. G. G/ 28/2/12

'The man has the political judgment of a flea.'   Dalton on Cripps.
Diary, 23 January 1939

'Your reticence and caution in the past has denoted a great patience – it
would be well for the "Fire-Eaters" to realise that 90% of
cannon-fodder would be made up of workers dead.'   Ben Tillett to
Neville Chamberlain, 7 February 1939. NC 7/11/32/253

By common consent, far the most urgent and important political questions
which confronted British politicians in the latter part of 1938 concerned
the linked problems, of foreign policy and defence. The post-Munich
'inquest' had revealed profound differences of opinion within all three
Parties, and there was good reason for thinking that these differences
existed at all levels of society. Conservative critics of the Government,
however, were far more prominent and influential than Opposition
politicians who upheld the Appeasement policy. On the face of it,
therefore, there was everything to be said for the Government's critics
making common cause. By their own analysis, the application of those
policies on which they agreed offered the sole chance of averting war; or, if
war was already inevitable, the best chance of averting defeat. Inevitably,
many minds turned to the possibility of creating some kind of 'Popular
Front', encompassing Labour, the Liberals, and Conservative critics of the
Government.

At the 1935 General Election, the National Government had secured a
majority well in excess of 250 over all opponents combined. By far the
largest Opposition party was Labour, which had won 154 seats. The
Labour Party, though substantial in numbers, was astonishingly short of
administrative experience. They had held office as recently as 1931; yet not
one of the principal members of that Government was currently available
to take senior office. Most of the leaders had defected to the National
Government; nearly all of those who did not defect were defeated at the
General Election a few weeks later. Only one member of the Labour

Cabinet survived the maelstrom: George Lansbury. *Faute de mieux*, he was chosen leader; but he was driven to resign in 1935, and was obviously out of sympathy with the general outlook of his Party on foreign affairs. Clement Attlee then became leader in Lansbury's place; but he was unimpressive and his leadership was often called into question. Herbert Morrison, who had played a major part on the London County Council, was regarded as a serious challenger.

By rather a curious contrast, the Liberals, with fewer than twenty seats, had several active members with Cabinet experience. The fame of Lloyd George – still in the Commons – towered above all others; but there were five men still active in Liberal politics who had served in Asquith's Cabinet before the war, and the Party Chairman, Sir Archibald Sinclair, had been briefly a member of the national Government Cabinet in 1931–2.

There remained two minor Opposition Parties. The Independent Labour Party (I.L.P.) held four seats, all in Glasgow, but had little influence or support elsewhere. The Communists had one M.P., sitting for a Scottish mining constituency; elsewhere, they enjoyed a considerable amount of sympathy among ostensible supporters of the Labour party, but very few votes.

Both the Labour and Liberal Parties had a recent history of bitter internal disagreements on political and personal grounds. For Labour in particular, the formation of the 1931 National Government had been a most traumatic experience: their spokesmen usually referred to it as 'the MacDonald betrayal'. The record of the Party on international questions had been turbulent. Most Labour M.P.s had supported the 1914 war, but a substantial minority had taken a pacifist line. In the 1920s and early 1930s there had been a strong vein of pacifism; and from this tradition it was not easy for Labour to escape. The embarrassing comments of Lansbury and Lord Noel-Buxton in 1938 have already been noted. Lord Ponsonby, another member of the small band of Labour peers, was a prominent sponsor of the extreme pacifist Peace Pledge Union ('I renounce war and will never support or sanction another'). Other Labour supporters were known for their sympathy with the cause of the Sudetendeutsch: another hangover from the 1920s, when it was fashionable in Labour circles to condemn Versailles and all its works. Only with great difficulty had the Labour Party been brought to accept the need for rearmament, and military conscription was still anathema. Even those Labour men who were by no means pacifists often showed little sense of proportion when viewing the prevailing dangers. They luxuriated in indignation over Spain, over Abyssinia and over the Japanese invasion of China; it took them a long time to perceive that Hitler was incomparably the biggest danger, and that some very unpalatable methods might be necessary if he was to be restrained. Yet when they were suddenly confronted with the German danger, the Labour Party reacted in a highly emotional manner. In the middle of the Czechoslovak crisis of September

1938, George Dallas of the T.U.C. exploded over the Foreign Secretary, 'Lord Halifax, listening to you we are ashamed to be Britishers!'[1] One may read the account of that interview in the Prime Minister's papers, or in the papers of Labour's Hugh Dalton; neither account seems to provide any basis for such an outburst, but it is symptomatic of the emotional, even personal, approach which Labour took over foreign policy.

The Liberals had their own troubles. They also had suffered serious defections among their leadership in 1931. At the end of 1938, four of the 'Liberal Nationals' who had seceded at that time were in the Cabinet, and others held more junior Government posts. Those who remained in the Liberal Party were not always on good terms with each other. Lloyd George's relations with Sir Archibald Sinclair were described as 'friendly, but not close'.[2] It was actually Chamberlain who called Lloyd George 'that unscrupulous little blackguard'[3] – but a large body of Liberals would have cheered that statement to the echo, had they known of it. Lloyd George had come to detest Viscount Samuel. Shortly after Munich, he sent an astonishing letter to Lord Mottistone,[4] full of the most bitter polemic against a man who, long before, had been a colleague of both sender and recipient, in Asquith's Cabinet. Lloyd George both received and transmitted invective which today seems difficult to comprehend.

Samuel's remarkable stand over Munich was by no means unique within his Party. The publicist Francis Hirst recorded his regret 'that Sinclair should have denounced Chamberlain for the one great and noble act of life'.[5] The Liberal Marquess of Lothian expressed views about Germany which make him the preceptor rather than the pupil of Sir Nevile Henderson, to whom he addressed them.[6]

It is perhaps tempting today to overestimate the authority of the Government's Conservative critics. Eden's reputation at the time was built largely on the circumstances of his resignation; he had done little as Foreign Secretary which made him appear an implacable opponent of Nazi Germany, while his attitude to Italy appears curiously emulative of the French. Winston Churchill seemed to speak with great knowledge, and it appeared to some that he had special sources of information. This matter has recently come under considerable discussion, and a good deal of evidence has been adduced about these sources.[7] Some influential contemporaries, however, doubted the existence of such sources.[8] One receives the uncomfortable impression that Churchill's conviction that the European Powers could be organised to contain Hitler was largely based on a considerable overestimate of French military power, and will to resist.

For years, these miscellaneous and frequently quarrelling critics posed no real threat to the Government, which therefore did not experience the sort of challenge which keeps administrations on their toes; while, conversely, the Opposition lacked the immediate expectation of office which conduces to responsible criticism. Could the critics nevertheless be welded together somehow to form a credible alternative Government?

The idea of a 'Popular Front' against the Government was widely discussed in 1937. The great advocate of the proposal was Sir Stafford Cripps, Solicitor-General in the Second Labour Government and a man generally considered to stand well to the left of his Party. Cripps's plan had been to link the I.L.P. and the Communists to Labour, thus providing a bloc similar to the current Government of France, and to the Spanish Government which was facing the challenge of Franco. Continental conditions, however, were profoundly different from those in Britain – not least in the comparative strengths of the Communist Parties – and the idea was turned down by an overwhelming majority at the Labour Party's Bournemouth Conference in October 1937.

The resignation of Eden in February 1938 made people think of a much broader kind of Popular Front: one which would include the Liberals, and the Conservative critics of the Government as well. In the spring of 1938, Cripps and his Labour associates sent a memorandum to their party's National Executive, arguing that 'an effective victory by the Labour Party alone is highly improbable at the next election.' The only way to overthrow the Government was 'to rally the unattached and politically unconscious voters of all shades of progressive opinion and of all classes by the demand for the formation of a new and more real national unity.'[9] Cripps's new proposal was rejected: the general view of Labour's National Executive was that if a Popular Front of that kind were formed, many members of the Labour Party itself would defect, and the loss of strength which would result would be greater than any gain from the other places. The Popular Front idea, however, was taken up with enthusiasm by the pro-Labour Sunday newspaper, *Reynold's News*. The National Executive took the challenge sufficiently seriously to send a stern and condemnatory letter to affiliated organisations; but many of these dissented from the official view and resolutions to the opposite effect began to pour into the Party's office.[10]

Liberal interest in the Popular Front began to become significant about the time of Eden's resignation. The Party's official line in support of Eden was by no means unanimous. Old-fashioned radicals with more than a streak of pacifism – like F. A. Hirst and J. A. Spender – contended that the line taken by Eden increased the risk of war. Other Liberals, like Lord Lothian, who were by no means pacifists, disliked it on very different grounds.[11] All, no doubt, were 'influential' men; but, unlike Sinclair, they were hardly charismatic, and did not sit in the House of Commons.

Even Sinclair was at first a little chary about the Popular Front. 'I agree with you', he wrote on 1 March 1938 to a close friend and political adviser, 'that Cripps has not got much chance of success – that is obviously an argument against our committing ourselves to him as a Party, but also an argument for giving him as much help, short of that, as we can.'[12] The Liberal press, however, reacted with similar enthusiasm to *Reynold's News*:

both the *Manchester Guardian* and the *News Chronicle* rendered eager support to the Popular Front.[13] In May, Sinclair gave the idea his public blessing, and it was widely taken up by Liberal parliamentarians. Sir Francis Acland, M.P. for a West Country constituency, wrote wistfully in June, 'Can't we force an election in the autumn and get them out and have a Lib-Lab-Eden-Cranborne Cabinet? . . . Surely the Popular Front idea is *really* on the move . . .'[14] All this turned on reciprocity from Labour and the Conservative rebels; and Labour in particular could only override the sense of its Bournemouth Conference and the deep suspicions of its organisers if something exceedingly important happened.

During the September crisis, the Government needed at times to discuss matters of national importance with its various critics; but it dealt with the individuals and bodies concerned separately and not collectively. The critics themselves do not appear to have coordinated strategy across Party barriers. The first sign of any real coming-together was in the immediate aftermath of Munich, and it was an empirical response to a political danger rather than to the international situation.

On 3 october, after the first day of the great debate in the House of Commons, Harold Macmillan approached Dalton, and told him that he and the other Conservative rebels feared that the Government would call an early General Election, during which the critics would be attacked by their own party organisation. Dalton was whisked off by taxi to a meeting with Macmillan, Churchill, Eden, Brenden Bracken and J. P. L. Thomas. According to Dalton's account,

> They spoke of the possibility of twenty or thirty of them being victimised and on the chance of some agreement with us for mutual support in the constituencies. I said that it was difficult to discuss anything of this kind at present and there were obvious snags, but if things went that way we might speak of it again later.[15]

Cripps had larger ideas. Three days later he met Dalton, and was told of the meeting with the Conservative rebels. Cripps now proposed that Attlee, Dalton and Morrison should meet three or four rebel Conservatives, and perhaps Sinclair as well. Dalton was non-committal, but thought the idea worth considering further. Later in the day, he contacted Attlee and Morrison, who were initially rather well-disposed. He then reported back to Macmillan, who

> was pleased at this but said that there was some difficulty within their group at present, Eden and others being very moderate and talking about national unity with everybody, while Winston and Duff Cooper were out for Chamberlain's blood and inclined to join with anybody else to get it . . . It was left that we should get in touch against next week.[16]

The contrast between the two leading Conservative rebels was very sharp. Churchill smouldered about the 'muffs and boobies' who had 'thrown away' the 'glorious victory' of 1918.[17] Eden, on the other hand, was actively seeking reconciliation with the Government less than a fortnight after Munich. On 11 October he had a long interview with Halifax, whom he told 'that he agreed with 90% of [Chamberlain's] position in [his] last speech in the House of Commons and would have voted with the Government – had it not been for his feeling of obligation to those with whom he had been working.'[18]

Eden's position, however, was crucial for the Conservative rebels. On 12 October, Dalton recorded:

> Macmillan is much disappointed with Eden, and does not know what he is playing at . . . Many of the Tory critics, however, are followers of Eden, and will not move further or faster than he. Churchill, on the other hand, is in danger of relapsing into a self-complacent Cassandra . . . Duff Cooper, who is much more of a fighter than Eden, thinks of himself as the man who might build a bridge between the latter and Churchill, and so unite and energise the Tory rebels. Macmillan himself would like to see a '1931 in reverse', that is, a breakaway from the Conservative Party and a union of Labour, Liberal and Tory dissidents to form a new 'national government.'[19]

Such aspirations, however, were hardly realistic without Eden, and contacts between Labour and dissident Conservatives became less frequent. What happened instead was a new kind of test for the Popular Front idea.

Although it is very easy to overstate the significance of parliamentary by-elections, they nevertheless provide some indication of the way public opinion is running. Several by-elections of the period help us to gauge whether the notion of inter-party cooperation against the Government had struck deep roots.

Oxford City was the first constituency to be contested after Munich. The seat was Conservative, but a Liberal had sat there for a time in the 1920s. In 1935, the Conservatives had a comfortable majority against Labour in a straight fight; in the next few years the town was a centre of Popular Front agitation.

Patrick Gordon-Walker, who had fought on Labour's behalf in 1935 and was still in the field, expected to be readopted. A remarkable revolt of the local Labour Party suddenly took place and – against the advice of their national organisers – they resolved to support instead A. D. Lindsay, Master of Balliol. Lindsay was a member of the Labour Party, but proposed to stand as an Independent, with backing also from the Liberals[20] and other supporters of the Popular Front. The Conservative defender was Quintin Hogg, son of Viscount Hailsham. The contest was seen by both sides as a vote of confidence, or otherwise, in the Government's foreign policy. The result, however, was an anticlimax. Hogg held the seat, but with a diminished majority. The Government had not won the clear demonstration of public support it had desired; its opponents had not proved any great revulsion from Munich, or that a candidate receiving support from both Opposition Parties would attract the huge vote which some Popular Front enthusiasts imagined.

Most other by-elections of the autumn were even less convincing than Oxford, and seemed to demonstrate very little more than the ordinary 'swing of the pendulum' which had been apparent long before Munich – certainly nothing approaching a landslide either way. Only one autumn result really called for comment, or provided indication of a possible change in public attitudes: Bridgwater. At the General Election, a Conservative had held the seat with a substantial overall majority in a three-cornered contest, the Liberal running slightly ahead of Labour. Vernon Bartlett, of the *New Chronicle*, one of the best-known political commentators of the day and a Liberal in politics, entered the contest with Liberal backing. The local Labour Party showed no enthusiasm to oppose him.[21] Thus Bartlett had a straight fight against the defending Conservative without presenting agonies of decision for the Labour Party; and on 17 November he took the seat, polling six thousand votes more than Liberals and Labour combined had done three years earlier.

Right at the end of the year, another by-election provided a different test: Kinross and West Perthshire. The Duchess of Atholl had held the seat as a Conservative in 1935 in a straight fight with a Liberal, Mrs Coll Macdonald. The Duchess, who was a keen supporter of the 'official' Spanish Government, decided to resign her seat and defend it at a by-election. An official Conservative was nominated against her. Popular Front theory presumably required that Mrs Coll Macdonald should withdraw, so that the Duchess should poll all the anti-Government vote.

Mrs Coll Macdonald, who probably had hopes of winning the seat, was by no means willing to comply with this suggestion, but after immense pressure from Sinclair and other Party notables she eventually stood down. Even this was hardly satisfactory from Sinclair's point of view; as he wrote:

> There was some slight difficulty in adjusting the statements to the Press afterwards, because whereas I wanted to make it clear that the whole object of Mrs. Coll Macdonald standing down was to ensure an emphatic vote against Mr. Chamberlain's foreign policy, the dominant consideration in Mrs. Coll Macdonald's mind was obviously the defeat of the Duchess![22]

Labour did not stand, and the Duchess had her straight fight; but the Government held Kinross on a reduced majority.

Early in 1939, a vacancy occurred at Holderness, where a Liberal had run second to the Conservative in 1935. There was another triangular contest at the by-election, but the Liberal, Aline Mackinnon, received public support from a number of prominent Labour people.[23] This does not seem to have had much effect on the result; the Conservative was again returned, and the gap between Liberal and Labour was not much altered. Meanwhile, the run of by-elections which were held in more ordinary political conditions told exactly the same story as the by-elections of late 1938: a continuing, but by no means overwhelming, swing against the Government – almost exactly as it had been before Munich. One is left with the firm impression that the great events of September 1938 exerted little effect on ordinary voting patterns. Bridgwater was evidently a flash in the pan, and may well repay more detailed study.

Sir Stafford Cripps did not abate his Popular Front agitation. In 1939 – which looked like a possible General Election year – this campaign had become a serious embarrassment to Labour, because the existence of the campaign implied – and many of its supporters positively stated – that Labour could not hope to win a General Election without some kind of Popular Front support: a contention which could hardly fail to give comfort to the Government and to demoralise local workers for the Labour Party.

In January 1939 the matter came to a head. Cripps requested a meeting of the Labour Party's National Executive, to discuss his Popular Front proposals. The meeting decided by seventeen to three against him; but Cripps immediately circulated local Labour bodies with his own arguments. A few days later another Labour Party Executive meeting was held, where views ranged from all-out support for Cripps on one side, to a proposal to expel him on the other, with considerable support for the idea of a special conference to resolve the matter one way or the other.[24] Finally – after what seems to have been a somewhat confused meeting – the National Executive of the Labour Party decided, on 25 January, to expel him from the Party altogether.

Predictably, an angry campaign for Cripps's reinstatement was promptly launched. Equally predictably, Labour's official organ tried to play down the extent of the pro-Cripps movement in the Party. 'It's a flop!' declared the *Daily Herald*,[25] 'Of the 613 Borough and Division Labour Parties 42 support the Cripps memorandum. One fifteenth. Of some 2,250 local parties, 35 support the memorandum. One sixty-fourth . . .' That leading article was somewhat tendentious; yet it would be difficult to deny that the impetus of the Popular Front had largely departed.

The Liberals had been much more enthusiastic for the Popular Front than Labour; but as time went on some of them began to have second thoughts. 'In London,' wrote a spokesman of the London Liberal Party, 'the key points are the seats that have been captured from us by the Labour Party after campaigns of a particularly objectionable kind.'[26] A number of working-class London seats had returned Liberals within the decade, and S. W. Bethnal Green was still Liberal. The very active candidate for one of those constituencies – David Goldblatt of Whitechapel – threatened to resign his candidature. Sinclair, anxious to avert such an event, gave a frank assessment of the Popular Front's prospects as they stood in March

1939: 'The most that is likely to happen would be an agreement on seats which would obviously not extend to places where the Tory vote is negligible. At any rate the movement is a long way from producing any results at all.'[27] The idea of electoral arrangements in a few crucial constituencies was much older and much more realistic than that of a nation-wide all-party campaign against the Government, which had fascinated Cripps a few months earlier.

As for the Conservative rebels, they went very much as Dalton had guessed. Churchill was a lonely figure, held rather at arm's length by some of the heterodox, as well as the orthodox, within his Party. By April 1939, Eden and Cranborne could hardly be called rebels at all; they were 'saying that there is no difference between them and the Government'.[28] The Popular Front idea was really dead, though nobody bothered to give it decent burial. King Party still sat on his throne.

9 Danger Signals

Q. 'What is the difference between Mr Chamberlain and Hitler?'
A. 'Mr Chamberlain takes his week-ends in the country; Hitler takes his countries in the week-ends.'   Riddle, c.1939

In the last three months of 1938, there were not many facts about the international situation which could really be cited as convincing evidence that Chamberlain's hopes at Munich had been vain; but it was difficult to deny that contacts between the Western Democracies and the Axis Powers were becoming tense and difficult; while a mass of rumour began to accumulate which suggested that the danger of war was close. At the end of the year, the British Military Attaché in Paris recorded the impression 'that the French General Staff are quite convinced that war is coming in Europe, and before very long'.[1] Cabinet papers, the correspondence of statesmen and diplomats, the tone of the newspapers, all suggest that this unhappy view was becoming more and more general. On 19 January Halifax circulated his own opinion to the Foreign Policy Committee of the Cabinet: 'There is one general tendency running through all the reports, and it is impossible, therefore, to ignore them. All the reports show that Hitler is contemplating another *coup* early this year, the danger period beginning towards the end of February.'[2] On 2 February, the Foreign Secretary went further, telling the Cabinet 'that the present state of tension could not last indefinitely and must end either in war or in the destruction of the Nazi regime.'[3] It is not astonishing that Oliver Stanley strongly concurred; what is really remarkable is that nobody in the Cabinet seems to have taken issue with that opinion. Sir Alexander Cadogan — Chamberlain's 'sane, slow man' — wrote to Halifax:

> I have the profoundest suspicion of Hitler's intentions. I believe that they are strictly dishonourable, and I believe what he would like best, if he could do it, would be to smash the British Empire . . . The only thing certain in a very uncertain world is that we must be prepared as best we can for anything.'[4]

Vansittart at his most caustic could not have improved on that.

Yet it is all too easy to read history backwards. We now know that Hitler's first act of international aggression after Munich was directed against the remains of Czechoslovakia. Was it not evident to all men that if Germany did strike, the Czechs must be the first victims?

This was by no means clear at the time. On 24 January 1939, Halifax sent a message to British diplomats in Washington, indicating that signs of a further German adventure in the spring of 1939 had been gradually becoming more definite ever since November. First indications had suggested the Ukraine as a likely direction of attack.[5] As Germany had no common frontier with the Ukraine, such a project necessarily implied either a prior attack on Poland or collaboration with Poland; and the possibility of a concerted German – Polish move in that direction came under discussion. British diplomats, however, appreciated that Poland's independent existence depended on her remaining at peace with both neighbours; war against either of them, even a victorious war, would upset the balance and set her own survival in jeopardy. Besides, she had minority problems enough already, without desiring gratuitously and at great risk to acquire more.[6] This suggested Poland herself as a possible victim.

There was also considerable discussion of a possible German attack on Holland. This danger was taken immensely seriously in Britain; noticeably less so by the Dutch themselves. An anxious paper on the subject was drawn up by the Cabinet's Foreign Policy Committee in January.[7] German moves in that direction might be aimed at a direct assault on the United Kingdom, perhaps by-passing France entirely.

Many other possible directions of German attack were considered. In 1919, the German towns of Danzig and Memel had been lopped from the Reich. Currently, Memel was Lithuanian, while Danzig was a Free City under League of Nations control – so maintained in order to ensure a good port through which Poland might have access to the sea. Even Henderson did not doubt that both places would soon fall into German hands.[8] A possible attack on Switzerland was discussed.[9] Perhaps Italy would be pushed to assert her claim against France to the point of war, and Germany would thus be assured of her somewhat hesitant ally's support from the start. Perhaps there would be 'impossible colonial demands'.[10] Cambon, French Ambassador in London, delivered himself of the opinion that Romania was the real danger spot.[11] The whole question was highly speculative; the one sombre fact which became increasingly clear even to those who had long nourished delusions about Hitler's intentions was that Germany was far from the end of her aggressive designs. Up to the time of Munich, the question usually asked in British official circles was whether war could be averted on reasonable terms; three or four months afterwards, the question was how best to prepare for a war which most informed people were coming to regard as inevitable.

On that assumption, the old question of coordination with France involved further diplomatic consultations, but a great deal more as well. Various difficulties, both old and new, were raised. Not least of these difficulties was the virtual certainty of leakage. The French press, as we have had much reason to observe, always regarded a news scoop as more important than the security of the State; there were leakages in other directions as well. One French newspaper proprietor believed that Léger was 'in the pay of the Soviets'.[12] A note communicated by Inskip to the Foreign Office in November 1938 warned them that 'there is a persistent leak of French Cabinet secrets into Germany. This is so serious in the view of my informant who, I may say, is a very highly placed person indeed, that nearly everything about France is known in Germany as the situation develops.'[13]

Britain and France had long adopted noticeably different attitudes to Mediterranean questions. The French were far more disposed than the British to regard Italy as a certain enemy if war came, and this conviction was no doubt to a measure self-serving. They also convinced themselves that Italy's support for General Franco was largely motivated by a desire to acquire Italian bases in Spain. In January 1939 the French even had the astonishing idea of seizing Minorca, 'so as to have some bargaining counter with which to induce the Italians to leave Majorca'.[14] Early in 1939, however, it became apparent that the Spanish Civil War was at last grinding to its conclusion, and the question arose whether to recognise Franco's administration as the lawful Government of Spain. By that time, the one chance for Dr Negrin's Government in the peninsula was that general war would break out quickly, and the Spanish conflict become merged in the wider struggle. Negrin actually admitted to the French Ambassador that this was his hope.[15] By the beginning of February Halifax had no remaining doubts about the issue of the Spanish Civil War, and told the Cabinet his own view that Britain 'should get some value out of recognising General Franco'.[16] The French had long demurred, but Bonnet reached the same conclusion as Halifax: recognition of Franco would give him 'a chance to get rather freer from Italy and Germany'.[17] This attitude, however, brought the British Government into bitter conflict with the Labour Opposition. To a large section of the Labour and even Liberal intelligentsia (though far less to the Labour working class) Spain was a profoundly 'charged' subject, and remained so long after the situation was irremediable. Almost three weeks later, when nobody could have doubted that the end of the Civil War, and the complete victory of Franco, were very close, Chamberlain wrote with some irritation to his sister about the 'really pathetic' demand of the Labour Party for arms for Government Spain, and Labour's protests against recognition of Franco.[18] Simultaneous recognition of Franco by the Western Democracies was eventually secured, though not without trouble. German and Italian troops were eventually withdrawn, and no attempt was made to retain military and naval bases. On that matter, at least, Mussolini kept his promise, and those who relied upon that promise were justified by later events. The last thing that Franco wanted when war eventually came was to be dragged into somebody else's struggle.

Military problems which confronted Britain and France presented greater difficulties than these diplomatic questions. At the time of the

September crisis great doubts had been cast on France's striking power, but it was generally agreed that she had a good chance of defending herself against attack. Now this too was called into question. In December 1938 Vansittart sent Halifax a most depressing analysis of the current situation.

When you and I were in Paris recently I noticed that M. Daldier spoke of France's ability to mobilise 100 divisions. This belongs to the same realm as his undertaking to produce 400 aeroplanes a month by next spring. France could not possibly mobilise or maintain 100 divisions. Our War Office, in several appreciations in the past, have estimated that the French could mobilise 53 divisions; but that owing to the exigencies of industrial production she could not maintain in the field much above 43 divisions.[19]

Vansittart went on to argue that Germany would soon be able to mobilise 150 divisions; that Italy, with a rather more numerous population than France, could put at least as many divisions in the field as her north-western neighbour. Thus France 'would be outnumbered by well over four to one on a conservative computation'. If Britain could only offer assistance to France on the scale which had been available in September, then – argued Vansittart – one of three things must happen: '(1) France might fight and be crushed by superior man power, (2) she might continue her disastrous policy of 1938, which consisted in bluffing and then running away when the real test came; (3) she might make her own terms with Berlin.' Vansittart was prone to exaggerate, and his figures are not always reliable in detail; but it is difficult to escape the general drift of his argument.

Nor was the Diplomatic Adviser alone. The British Military Attaché in Paris warned that 'as a result of recent changes in Europe, particularly in Czechoslovakia, the French military authorities do not consider that France is now in a position to defend herself against Germany without military assistance from the United Kingdom.'[20] Such warnings could hardly have been expressed more forcefully without spreading complete defeatism in the Allied camp. Mere defence of the Western Democracies from attack, let alone a foreign policy designed to contain Germany in the east, presupposed as an essential ingredient a substantial contribution of forces from Britain.

Vansittart continued to bombard the Foreign Secretary with missives in the same vein. Halifax at last returned an almost plaintive reply: 'What can we do? I am quite willing to bring the matter under formal consideration of the C.I.D. or Cabinet – but hesitate to do so unless I can make some constructive proposal.'[21] This gave Vansittart his opening. 'It should be made at once clear to the Cabinet that Anglo-French relations will be in severe danger and the capacity of French resistance will rapidly be exhausted unless we greatly increase our military contribution.'

Cadogan added a minute of his own, more mildly expressed than the other, but not differing in its message.[22]

What, then, should Britain do to rectify the situation? The French view was clear enough: they wanted Britain to introduce compulsory military service. That opinion had long been implicit; Daladier stated it explicitly to Phipps towards the end of January.[23] Conscription, however, was a political hornets' nest, and any move in that direction could well do far more harm than good. The Chief of the Imperial General Staff himself was compelled to accept the view that 'an army on a continental scale' was 'beyond our resources in peace'.[24]

If the Army was not designed to act as a major force in a European war, then what was it designed to do? In December 1937 the Cabinet 'defined the priorities which were to govern the state of preparedness of the army.'[25] They were – in order of precedence – preserving internal security of the United Kingdom; protection of the country and its trade routes against external attack; defence of British territories overseas; and, finally, 'our fourth objective, which can only be provided after the other objectives have been met, is cooperation in the defence of the territories of any allies we may have in war.' A possible offensive role was not even mentioned.

According to plans which were still current at the end of 1938, two regular divisions and one mobile division, with reserves, would be ready to embark for the continent at twenty-one days' notice. Forty days from the origin of an emergency, another two regular divisions, with war reserves at about half the scale of the first two, would be ready to join them. No further divisions would be available until ten months from the emergency. All of these units would be equipped for defensive warfare only.

In December 1938, the Chief of the Imperial General Staff produced a paper, arguing for a modest reorganisation of this little army. The mobile division should be split into two smaller divisions. The four infantry divisions should 'have the equipment and war reserves necessary for war against a first-class Power in any part of the world.' According to the new proposals, the first two divisions of the Field Force thus constituted would be ready to embark within fourteen days of the emergency; thereafter, two additional divisions would embark at intervals of fourteen days until all six had embarked. Four Territorial divisions, with reserves and equipment, would be able to proceed overseas in four months from the onset of an emergency. Thus, in all, ten British divisions would be on the continent within six weeks.

The Cabinet examined the War Office proposals at the beginning of February 1939. It was impossible to deny that some extra Army expenditure would be necessary in the financial year 1939/1940; but both the Prime Minister and the Chancellor of the Exchequer were far from happy about the increases proposed. The necessary increase in the defence loan, argued Simon, would place severe strains on the pound. 'We might be faced with a financial crisis as grave as that of 1931, but with the added difficulty that the foreign situation was now far more serious.'[26] Halifax, however, came strongly to the support of Leslie Hore-Belisha, Secretary for War: 'We were borrowing in respect of a period which could not last indefinitely'.

Such arguments overbore opposition. Some of Hore-Belisha's proposals were accepted at once, others were eventually adopted with certain modifications. In particular, a rather small monetary saving was effected, at the cost of substantial delays in the schedule for despatch of troops to the continent. Once the Cabinet had reached agreement, however, there was no reason to fear parliamentary difficulties; for Hore-Belisha had noted a significant change in the House of Commons: 'Up to this year there had been no Parliamentary pressure in regard to the Field Force but pressure was now becoming evident.'[27] Eventual adoption of the army proposals was a foregone conclusion.

Now that Britain was proposing a substantial increase in her army, it became meaningful to consider staff conversations with the French which would cover the whole field of operations in which the two countries might find themselves working together in a future war. The instructions on the subject which were sent to Phipps on 3 February are illuminating, for they show the assumptions which were being made about probable enemies. Germany and Italy were both assumed to fall in that category; but Japan might be ignored, at least in the beginning, for she would 'be likely to adopt a cautious attitude' through her involvements in China, and fear both of the United States and of the Soviet Union.[28]

The French delayed their reply for a considerable time. More than a fortnight later, Halifax prodded Phipps to 'do what you can to expedite a reply'.[29] Eventually an affirmative answer came. Discussions about the level at which the conversations should be conducted, the need for secrecy, and the best venue, extended casually over the next few weeks. On 11 March the French proposed a date: 15 March. This, in the British view, was too soon. In any event, that day would witness events a good deal more spectacular than staff conversations.[30]

The very leisurely character of these proceedings may perhaps be related to a curious lull in the European situation which was noted in the late winter of 1938-9. On 25 January, Ogilvie-Forbes reported from Berlin that 'during the last two weeks there has been a considerable diminution of outspoken criticism in the German Press against us.'[31] In private, Chamberlain was very encouraged by the course of events. 'I myself begin to feel at last', he wrote to his sister on 5 February, 'that we are getting on top of the dictators. The situation is well put by Scrutator in the *Sunday Times* today. They missed (or rather Hitler missed) the bus last September and once you have done that in international affairs it is very difficult to reproduce the situation.'[32] 'According to my information,' he wrote to another sister a week later, 'Hitler and Ribbentrop so far from hatching schemes against us are snatching round for some means of approaching us without the dangers of a snub.'[33]

About this time Henderson, whose health had partially improved, returned to his post at Berlin. On 15 February, the Ambassador and the Duke of Coburg—a rather remote kinsman of the British Royal Family—both spoke at the Deutsch-Englische Gesellschaft dinner. The Duke's speech contained an encouraging reference to his belief that 'a new and fruitful element for cooperation between the two nations has been established'. This passage was widely noted by those who believed, or wished to believe, that cooperation was possible. Henderson had shown an advance copy of his own speech to the Duke; the Duke's speech was then 'completely rewritten under higher direction with result that it was only made available for His Royal Highness to read during the dinner itself.'[34] In Henderson's view, the crucial passages had 'received personal approval of Herr Hitler himself'.

The view that there had been a break in the clouds was not confined to the incorrigible optimists. On 7 March telegrams were sent to the Dominion Governments: '. . . We are now inclined to think that Hitler has for the time being abandoned the idea of precipitating an immediate crisis such as he seemed to be contemplating at the beginning of the year.'[35] Next day Halifax told the Cabinet of Ashton-Gwatkin's recent visit to Berlin, where he had met Ribbentrop and Göring: 'The atmosphere had been very friendly, and he had gained the impression that no immediate adventures of a large type were anticipated.'[36] Exactly a week after this comforting news was imparted, troops of the German Reich marched into the city of Prague.

10 The End of Czechoslovakia

'Like Chatham "I know that I can save this country and I do not believe that anyone else can".'   Neville to Ida Chamberlain, 12 March 1939. NC 18/1/1089

On 19 September 1938, the British Government offered to participate in a guarantee of the remainder of Czechoslovakia, provided that the Czechs agreed to cede the Sudetenland to Germany. The matter was discussed further at Munich. In an annex to the main agreement, the four Heads of Government acknowledged that

> His Majesty's Government . . . and the French Government have entered into the above agreement on the basis that they stand by the offer . . . of the 19th. September relating to an international guarantee of the new boundaries of the Czechoslovak State against unprovoked aggression. When the question of the Polish and Hungarian minorities in Czechoslovakia had been settled, Germany and Italy for their part will give a guarantee to Czechoslovakia.

The new state was, of course, completely indefensible from a military point of view, and its survival must depend either on the forebearance of neighbouring countries, or on the effectiveness of the guarantees as a deterrent. Sir Samuel Hoare was particularly optimistic about the prospect, stating in the House of Commons on 3 October that 'I believe that the guarantee, coupled, it may be, with pacts of non-aggression given by this country, France, Germany and Italy, with the minorities question settled in Czechoslovakia will make the new Republic as safe as Switzerland has been for many generations in the past on the continent of Europe.'

Why was this prophecy not fulfilled?

In the post-Munich debate in the two Houses of Parliament several other significant statements of British policy were made by senior members of the Cabinet. Inskip explained that

> the formal treaty of guarantee has yet to be drawn up . . . Until that has been done, technically, the guarantee cannot be said to be in force. His

Majesty's Government, however, feel under a moral obligation to
Czechoslovakia to treat the guarantee as being now in force. In the
event, therefore, of an act of unprovoked aggression against Czechoslovakia, His Majesty's Government would certainly feel bound to take all
steps in their power to see that the integrity of Czechoslovakia is
preserved.

Halifax admitted continuing doubts about the form of the guarantee:
'whether its form should be joint or several; what states should be invited to
assume its obligations; and in what circumstances these obligations should
be held to arise.' Sir Samuel Hoare and Sir John Simon – each a former
Foreign Secretary himself – made it clear that there was no desire to
exclude Russia from the arrangements.

The more thoroughly the question of guarantees came to be considered,
the more difficult it appeared. No fewer than nine countries were
mentioned from time to time as possible guarantors: the four Munich
Powers; the Soviet Union; Poland, Hungary, Romania, Yugoslavia. As
this list included all the states which bordered on Czechoslovakia, it was
obvious that any attack must come from one of the suggested guarantors;
hence, as Halifax observed in November, 'if all the states mentioned . . .
are to be guarantors it is obvious that a strictly joint guarantee, which
would only become operative if all the guarantors agreed to act, would,
from the point of view of Czechoslovakia, not be worth the paper it was
written on.'[1] At the other extreme, however, 'on geographical and
strategic grounds . . . a guarantee limited to say France and Great Britain
could probably not be effectively implemented in the present circumstances and for this reason would not act as a deterrent.' Several possible
ways out of the tangle were examined by the Foreign Secretary; but all of
them seemed to bristle with special difficulties of their own.

The question of the British guarantee was raised during the Paris visit of
Chamberlain and Halifax late in November. The usual diplomatic fencing
took place. Bonnet pointed out that Czechoslovakia had been led to
believe that it would receive a British guarantee; Chamberlain accepted
this, but retorted that the British Government had no intention of
incurring an obligation in Central Europe which might fall on Britain
alone: a proposition which had been clear all along. Halifax proposed a
guarantee by the four Munich Powers, which would only come into effect
if at least three of them agreed that unprovoked aggression had been
committed. The French, not suprisingly, were inclined to baulk at this
proposal. Suddenly Chamberlain had a brainwave: 'an idea', as he wrote
to his sister, 'which found immediate favour and at any rate for the time
being restored complete harmony.[2] The Prime Minister's proposal was
that the Czechs themselves should be asked whether they desired the
guarantee to take the form of the current British proposal.

The British Cabinet, however, was a good deal less enthusiastic about

Chamberlain's apparently felicitous solution. Sir Samuel Hoare wanted a military guarantee by Britain, France and the Soviet Union. Walter Elliot, Minister of Health thought it 'very undesirable' that Britain should exert 'pressure on the Czechoslovak Government to abandon Russia's guarantee to that country'.[3] In the end, however, the Cabinet accepted the idea of asking the Czechs their views on the matter, and then referring it to the Foreign Policy Committee, which was authorised to act in light of the reply.

This apparently simple solution proved a great deal more difficult than had appeared to be the case. Early in December, Newton saw Chvalkovsky, the new Czechoslovak Minister for Foreign Affairs, and discussed with him the possible form of guarantee. Chvalkovsky was guarded; but on one point he was clear and emphatic: 'the importance of giving the guarantees as soon as possible. Their form and extent were less important than promptitude.'[4] The French, who made similar inquiries of the Czechs, received similar answers. About that time, von Ribbentrop was visiting Paris, and was taxed by his hosts on the question of German participation in the guarantees. The attitude of the German Foreign Secretary was described as 'rather unsatisfactory'; apparently 'he said he thought she would prefer not to do so and indicated that the German Government were inclined to fear Czechoslovakia might relapse at some future date into an anti-German Beneš policy.[5] This differed significantly from the four-Power statement at Munich: that Germany and Italy would join in the guarantees once the question of Hungarian and Polish claims had been resolved. There is little indication, however, that the importance of the change was fully appreciated at the time.

The French attitude also underwent a sharp change. On 9 January 1939 Phipps reported that France would prefer a joint guarantee by the four Munich Powers.[6] The following day, Chamberlain and Halifax met Daladier and Bonnet while *en route* for Rome; the French explained that they sought a guarantee 'which would only come into play if three of the four guaranteeing Powers were in agreement'.[7] This was exactly what Chamberlain and Halifax had wanted in November, when the French demurred so strongly.

At Rome a day or so later, it was apparent that Italian opinion had also changed since Munich. Mussolini stalled a decision:

> It might be considered who was likely to attack Czechoslovakia. Not Poland: she was not likely to make any attack; not Romania, she had nothing to gain by it; not Hungary. He did not think Russia would attack, and Germany had shown that she regarded herself now as the protectress of Czechoslovakia; so that he did not think that it was likely that there would be an attack on her from any side.[8]

What possible harm, we might ask, could be done by the four Munich

Powers giving the guarantees which had been promised more than three months earlier?

The solemn negotiations—one is tempted to use the word 'farce'—continued. On 8 February Britain made a formal approach to the Germans. Reply was delayed for nearly three weeks: the eventual answer was that Germany would only consider giving such a guarantee if at least one of the other states bordering Czechoslovakia would undertake similar obligations.[9] This was very different from what Hitler had agreed at Munich: and the matter of the guarantee was in fact still under active discussion a week before the German occupation of Prague.[10]

While the question of the guarantees was agitating diplomats and politicians in Britain and France, the state whose existence they were proposing to assure was in the process of falling to pieces. The story of that disintegration is complex, but is of considerable relevance to the wider international issues involved, and in particular helps to explain the behaviour of all four Munich Powers during the middle of March.

German occupation of the Sudetenland had not been without incidents; but, on the whole, it had been humane and efficient, and the resistance offered to it minimal. Doubtful areas were allocated by international commission, not by plebiscite. The allocation, however, was a very one-sided affair; Chamberlain described it to the Cabinet as a 'compromise in which Czechoslovakia had ceded everything and gained nothing'.[11]

Much more trouble arose over other claimants to Czechoslovak territory. Just before midnight on 30 September—the very day on which the Munich agreement was signed—Poland sent a demand to Czechoslovakia for the prompt cession of Teschen and certain other territories. The British Ambassador in Warsaw remonstrated strongly, but before any possible effect of his *démarche* could be felt, Czechoslovakia accepted the ultimatum. Anticipating similar demands from Hungary, the Czechs on their own initiative offered negotiations.[12] With Germany and Italy as arbitrators, the frontier with Hungary was settled at the beginning of November. The new Czechoslovakia, however, was still not free from minority problems; for, apart from Czechs, Slovaks and Ruthenians, something like 378,000 Germans and 100,000 Magyars remained within her borders. On the other side, 738,000 Czechs and Slovaks passed to Germany, and 288,000 to Hungary. In the territory ceded to Poland, Czechs and Slovaks actually outnumbered Poles by more than two to one.[13]

How far most of the people of Czechoslovakia were moved by the tremendous events of September and the immediate aftermath is hard to say. There were many reports of distress among crowds in Prague; but people who demonstrate in cities are often unrepresentative of their nations. Even in the towns there were not many dramatic and violent gestures. The people, who had reposed such trust in their great allies, felt totally abandoned. As for the ordinary peasant, Newton reported on 22 October that his chief feeling was probably one of relief that he was not called upon to spill his blood . . . He has no great use for the politicians of the past regime, whom he regards largely as a band of robbers feathering their own nests, and his national feeling was, and is, far weaker than his interest in agricultural prices and in the rates of taxation.[14]

The first major political news from Czechoslovakia after Munich was the resignation of President Beneš, announced on 5 October. The slow machinery for choosing a successor lumbered into operation; meanwhile, the three Slavonic regions began to fall apart.

In Slovakia, continued Newton's October report, 'the People's Party [the old Hlinka Party] is apparently the only party that counts now and is gaining adherents daily. It is going ahead on fascist lines far more openly and obviously than the central government.' Hlinka himself was dead, and undergoing political apotheosis: a process always more safely applied to the dead than to the living, for the former cannot complain of activities performed in their name. Memory of the late priest was perpetuated in the designation of a para-military body, the Hlinka Guard. Leadership of the Slovak political movement passed rapidly to another priest, Dr Tiso.

Ruthenia also began to develop in a direction of its own. The rural population were Uniates: that is, their religious ritual resembled that of the Eastern Churches, but they were in communion with Rome. Before the War, only 17 per cent of the Ruthenians were literate; most of the literate minority seem to have been Magyar-speaking Jews who lived in the towns. Both Hungarians and Poles were anxious that Ruthenia should return to Hungary, thus establishing a common frontier between the two countries. At the end of October, the provincial administrator was charged with treasonable conspiracy with Hungarians and Poles. A successor was appointed: one Father Vološin, described as 'an elderly pedant, much more interested in his linguistic studies and the replacement of Hungarian by Ruthenian as the language of his country than in the business of governing.'[15]

Beneš, for all his faults, had been an impressive political figure. Among surviving politicians of his régime, none stood noticeably ahead of his fellows; but choice of a new President eventually alighted on Emil Hacha, a sixty-six year old lawyer of rather conservative proclivities. As the formation and preservation of Czechoslovakia had depended largely on the personalities of the country's first two presidents, it is scarcely surprising that political separatism soon became very important with a much less substantial figure at the helm. On 19 November the Chamber of Deputies voted by a large majority for Slovak and Ruthenian autonomy. Each of the two eastern provinces now found itself presided over by a priest with very little political experience, associated with ministers who had less experience still. In recognition of the new condition of the country, Czecho-Slovakia soon acquired a symbolic hyphen in its name.

It is not easy to decide how far the post-Munich disruption of Czecho-Slovakia was a spontaneous process, deriving from the many differences between Czechs, Slovaks and Ruthenians, and to what extent it was the artificial product of German propaganda and other German activities. Nor was it even certain in the early days that Germany desired the state to disintegrate. There were signs that the new administration was prepared to comply with known German wishes; the Communist Party was dissolved, and anti-Jewish measures were reported to be under contemplation – although there never seems to have been much enthusiasm for the latter policy. Disruption of Czecho-Slovakia would be likely to result in Ruthenia – perhaps Slovakia as well – becoming linked to Hungary, thus creating a potentially formidable Hungarian – Polish bloc. In spite of these possible early doubts however, the Germans seem have decided fairly soon in favour of encouraging disruption in Czecho-Slovakia.

Slovakia, which had none of the anti-German tradition of the Czechs, was particularly willing to comply with Hitler's wishes. At the Slmvak Diet elections on 18 December, the single list of candidates secured 98 per cent of the votes:[16] speedy emulation indeed of the pattern of overwhelming majorities characteristic of all totalitarian countries. The following month, four Slovak political parties whose activites had been suspended in the autumn were formally dissolved: the Communists, the Czecho-Slovak Social Democratic Party, the German Social Democratic Party and the Jewish Party.[17]

Some developments in Ruthenia resembled those in Slovakia, but others were noticeably different. The Prague Government behaved rather more toughly towards the small province, and incurred some local obloquy when it insisted on appointing the Czech General Lev Prchala as a member of the Ruthenian Government.[18] Information reaching the British Foreign Office indicated that the local people 'insofar as they are capable of thinking about the question at all . . . would probably like best to be a little independent state with unrestricted trade with and emigration to Hungary. Failing this, they would probably prefer annexation to Hungary.'[19] 'The real ruler of the country', added the report, 'is M. Billy, the Chief of Police . . . [who] exercises a virtual dictatorship.' At the Diet elections in January, the Ruthenians proved themselves rather less effective totalitarians than the Slovaks. The poll was over 90 per cent; but the single list – the 'Ukrainian Party of National Unity' – secured only 85 per cent of the votes cast, and 7 per cent had the temerity to vote against it.

Reports from the Czech lands to the west were of more doubtful import. Some moves in the fascist direction had already been made; but they were, by Central European standards of the time, very mild. In January Hitler subjected Chvalkovsky to a forty-minute 'interview', during which the Führer spoke for thirty minutes on end; largely in diatribe against the Jews. Chvalkovsky – according to the Czech Minister in Berlin – countered the suggestion that Czecho-Slovakia should imitate the German example by a very neat rejoinder: 'Czecho-Slovakia, not being a Great Power, could not adopt the German method.'[20] There were signs, however, that the Germans were not wholly satisfied with attitudes in Czecho-Slovakia. 'Contrary to all commonsense,' wrote Göring's newspaper, the *National Zeitung*, 'a section of the Czech press has adopted an unfriendly and occasionally even an arrogant tone towards Germany.'[21]

In the first week of March, the British Minister reported that 'relations between Czechs and Slovaks seem to be heading for a crisis.'[22] The nominal issue was financial. Czecho-Slovak finances had been in a precarious state ever since Munich, in spite of a large loan from Britain; and Slovakia was anxious to secure her share of whatever was going. 'The Czechs', wrote Newton, 'declared themselves prepared to give it subject to guarantees that the Slovaks intended to pursue a policy of loyalty to Czecho-Slovak state, a matter on which recent utterances of Slovak leaders left room for doubt.'

On 10 March it was reported that the Czecho-Slovak Government had dismissed Tiso, proscribed the Hlinka Guard and established martial law in the Slovak capital, Bratislava, in order to forestall a threatened coup by separatists.[23] That day even Sir Nevile Henderson began to take fright at the likely role of Germany in the developing situation: quoting with apparent concurrence the apprehensions of his Military Attaché lest 'some trouble between Czechs and Slovaks [should occur] such as will give the Germans an excuse for forcible interference.' He also recognised that 'if Herr Hitler seeks adventure the most obvious form which it would be likely to take would be some coup in Czecho-Slovakia'.[24]

Later that day, the Slovak crisis developed further. Sidor, another prominent Slovak minister who at one time had appeared particularly amenable to German wishes, was appointed premier in succession to Tiso, and at midnight 'stated on the wireless that the political situation would be cleared up and a new Government constitutionally appointed within the next few hours'.[25] As we shall shortly see, the course of events in Slovakia after this was largely misunderstood in London at the time; but we are indebted to Newton for an account written on 21 March which seems to set the record straight.[26]

Sidor returned to Bratislava the following day, 11 March. According to Newton's account, at about 10 p.m. that day Seyss-Inquart (who had played an important part in the Austrian *Anschluss* a year earlier) and Buerckel, another prominent Reich Nazi, walked into a Cabinet meeting in progress at Bratislava, accompanied by five German guards. The Nazis

> told the Slovak Government that they should proclaim the independence of Slovakia. When Monsieur Sidor showed hesitation, Herr Buerckel took him on one side and explained that Herr Hitler had decided to settle the question of Czecho-Slovakia definitely. Slovakia

ought therefore to proclaim her independence because Herr Hitler would otherwise disinterest himself in her fate. Monsieur Sidor thanked Herr Buerckel for this information, but said that he must discuss the situation with the Government at Prague.

Early on the following Sunday morning Monsieur Tiso requested that a meeting of the Cabinet should be held at 8 a.m. Monsieur Sidor agreed, but said that the meeting must not take place in the building ordinarily used because it was guarded by the German Ordner and was also too close to the bridge across the Danube. The Cabinet accordingly met in his private apartment . . . Tiso . . . said that he had received a telegram by the hand of Herr Buerckel inviting him to go at once to see the Führer in Berlin. He had to accept this invitation because Herr Buerckel had informed him that otherwise the two German divisions on the other side of the Danube would occupy Bratislava, and the Hungarians would be authorised to seize not only Ruthenia, as had already been agreed by Berlin, but also eastern Slovakia.

Tiso proposed to make a somewhat leisurely journey to Berlin, which would give the Slovak Government time to contact Prague and Warsaw. On arrival at Vienna, however, he was hustled into an aeroplane 'and informed that he was to proceed in it to Berlin at once as Herr Hitler awaited him.'

The following afternoon, Monday 13 March – so Newton's account goes – the Slovak Cabinet was in session, and received a telephone call in German from Tiso, saying that he was speaking from Berlin from the office of Hitler, with Ribbentrop, Neurath and General Brauchitsch also present. 'He had orders to request the Cabinet to summon a meeting of the Slovak Parliament for the following Tuesday morning at 10 a.m.'

Tiso returned to Bratislava in the small hours of 14 March. He explained to the Slovak Cabinet that Hitler had told him that Slovakia must proclaim her independence by midday, or he would 'disinterest' herself in her fate. When the deputies met, Tiso read them the text of proposed law proclaiming independence, 'which had been given to him by Herr von Ribbentrop already drafted in Slovak'. The deputies, naturally, wished to discuss the matter; but Karmasin, leader of the German minority, told Sidor that the Germans would begin to occupy the Czech town Moravska Ostrava at noon, 'and that he should be careful lest Bratislava suffered similar treatment'. The deputies 'protested in dismay and great distress at this treatment' – but complied with the German orders, and proclaimed independence.

The account of these events which was generally believed in Britain during the next few days suggested that Tiso's visit to Hitler had been on Slovak initiative; that the Slovak Parliament had been summoned by Hacha, President of the Republic; and that the declaration of independence had been the product of propaganda and subversion from

Germany, rather than threats. In Neville Chamberlain's account, given in the House of Commons on the afternoon of 15 March, for example, it was stated that 'Dr. Tiso appealed to Herr Hitler and received an official invitation to go to Berlin'. This makes Tiso appear, at best, extremely naive, and at worst a traitor. Newton's later account presents him in a very different light: a man who perhaps made the wrong decision, but who may certainly be excused for having made it. Again, the Prime Minister declared that 'the independence of Slovakia was proclaimed with the approval of the Diet'. 'Approval' is certainly not the appropriate word to describe reluctant concession to a threat of military occupation. Chamberlain gave the best factual account he could, in light of the information available to him; but anyone who toils through the diplomatic documents of the time will appreciate how extraordinarily difficult it was to sort out fact from rumour and propaganda.

It has often been assumed that the separation of Slovakia inevitably spelt disaster for the Czech lands to the west. This was not necessarily true. The Poles at any rate were disposed to believe that 'if Slovakia and Ruthenia attained their independence the Czecho-Slovak Government would be stronger and more capable of resisting German penetration.'[27] A strong argument could be advanced for the view that Slovakia and Ruthenia were economic and political liabilities; and that a more or less homogeneous Czech state of perhaps six or seven million people was not necessarily inviable.

On the afternoon of 14 March, shortly after the Slovak declaration, President Hacha and Foreign Minister Chavlkovsky left Prague for Berlin to meet Hitler. Here again the story of what happened was not known in detail for several days afterwards, and Chamberlain, speaking in the House of Commons almost immediately after the events, could give little useful information. Some details even now appear uncertain; but the story which emerged a few days later[28] indicates that, shortly after midnight, Hitler told the Czechs that he proposed to occupy Bohemia and Moravia the same morning, and incorporate them as a Protectorate of the German Reich. According to one account, the document declaring concession to the German demands was produced, ready for the Czechs' signatures; according to the German story, the wording was only agreed after discussion. In any event, Hitler soon left the room, with his officials still in conference with the Czechs. Hacha and Chvalkovsky protested, but were informed that 800 German bombers would depart 6 a.m. to bomb Prague unless the signatures had been received. Like Tiso, the Czech Ministers were given the opportunity to communicate by telephone with their Cabinet, which apparently concurred that opposition was impossible, and issued orders that the invading Germans should not be resisted. The required document was duly signed in Berlin. At least once during the ordeal, Hacha collapsed and required urgent medical attention; though whether this happened before or after he had appended his signature is a matter of conflict between the accounts.

At 6 a.m. on 15 March the general invasion began. German troops met practically no resistance, and in the course of the day occupied all Bohemia and Moravia. At least two towns had actually been seized the previous night, in anticipation of diplomatic procedures. Events of September and thereafter had resulted in the complete demoralisation of the country.

After Czecho-Slovakia was destroyed, the political condition of Slovakia and the Czech lands differed considerably. On the day of the invasion, Halifax discovered from the German Ambassador in London that Slovakia would 'enjoy independence, assisted economically and otherwise by Germany', while the Czechs, who came under Henlein as *Statthalter*, would merely 'not serve in the German army and would generally enjoy rights of self-government and natural development'.[29]

Just as great confusion attended those diplomatic events which preceded the extinction of Czecho-Slovakia, so also were observers from the West most undertain about the circumstances which accompanied the German occupation. *The Times*, for example, published an account in its issue of 23 March which reported over 18,000 arrests: a figure Newton considered 'may be pure guesswork'.[30] A fortnight after the annexation he expressed the opinion 'that the Gestapo are going about their business, at any rate in Prague, with greater circumspection than . . . certainly was anticipated by the Czech population'. Newton inclined, however, to the view 'that the situation becomes progressively worse the greater the distance from Prague'. Synagogues had been burnt at Brünn and Olmutz; none thus far in the capital.

In the short period between the Slovak declaration of independence and the German occupation of Bohemia and Moravia, Hungary issued an ultimatum to the Czech Government to withdraw troops from Ruthenia. Prchala compiled,[31] and Hungarians began to cross the frontier. While this was happening, Vološin took occasion to declare the independence of his tiny country, with the sonorous title of the State of Carpatho-Ukraine.[32] Invading Hungarians met considerable resistance, both from Czechs and from local 'Sitsch' guards, and about fifty Hungarians were reported killed.[33] The most serious obstacle to their progress, however, seems to have been the peculiarly foul weather, and it was not until 16 March that they reached the Polish frontier. By that time a further hazard had been introduced into the situation, for the Romanians proceeded to demand a slice of Ruthenia, and on 20 March 30,000 Hungarians and 40,000 Romanians were reported to be facing each other in an obviously tense situation.[34]

Rumour and speculation of the wildest kind was rife. In particular, there were conflicting views on Germany's role in Ruthenia and her attitude to Hungary. The European situation was about as confused as it has ever been in modern history, and the more closely men looked into it the more uncertain the indications became.

11 Preparing for the Inevitable

ἐν δε ταῖς Ἀθήναις τῆς Παράλου ἀφικομένης νυκτὸς ἐλέγετο ἡ συμφορά,
καὶ οἰμωγὴ ἐκ τοῦ Πειραιῶς διὰ τῶν μακρῶν τειχῶν εἰς ἄστυ διῆκεν,
ὁ ἕτερος τῷ ἑτέρῳ παραγγέλλων· ὥστ᾽ ἐκείνης τῆς νυκτὸς οὐδεὶς
ἐκοιμήθη, οὐ μόνον τοὺς ἀπολωλότας πενθοῦντες, ἀλλὰ πολὺ μᾶλλον
ἔτι αὐτοὶ ἑαυτούς ...

'When the Paralos arrived in Athens by night the news was told; and
a wailing surged out of the Piraeus through the long walls into the
city, as one told the news to another; and that night no one slept, not
only lamenting those who had perished, but much more for
themselves ...'   Xenophon, Hellenica 2, ii, 3, describing how the
Athenians received news of the decisive defeat at Aegospotami

It is almost impossible to overstate the measure of sheer uncertainty about
facts – let alone the interpretation of those facts – which overhung not
merely the Western Powers but almost everybody else on 15 March 1939.
Even Mussolini had apparently received no prior intimation of what
Hitler proposed to do. As we have already seen, on at least two important
questions where the Prime Minister ventured a factual statement to the
House of Commons, later information showed that he was wrong. There
was no doubt that German troops were pouring over the frontier into
Bohemia and Moravia, and meeting little or no resistance, and that Hacha
and Chvalkovsky had been closeted with the Nazi leaders during the small
hours of the morning; but, beyond that, practically nothing was known for
certain in Britain. Had there been some kind of invitation from the Czech
Government, conceivably to forestall a coup? It appeared that Hungary
was sending troops into Ruthenia, and the Cabinet was told that Romania
was doing the same.[1] Were the two countries in collusion with Germany
and each other, or were they acting to forestall Germany, or each other, or
both?

By coincidence, the regular weekly meeting of the Cabinet was held on
the morning of the invasion, and the minutes of that meeting underline the
uncertainty. Yet one very thorny problem arose. Was Britain under some
sort of moral obligation to intervene, in the light of what had been said on

the guarantee question just after Munich? That she was powerless to do anything which would save the immediate situation was patent to all; but was there some sort of quixotic duty to declare war on Germany – conceivably on Hungary as well? In fact there was no political pressure for immediate action, either in Britain or in France; but Chamberlain could not have known that at the time. He decided – and the Cabinet agreed with him – that the proposed guarantees could not be invoked, because 'the state whose frontiers we had undertaken to guarantee against unprovoked aggression had now completely broken up.'

The Labour Opposition demanded an immediate Parliamentary debate – a demand which could scarcely be resisted, though it was difficult to see what good it would do. Chamberlain did the only thing possible that afternoon. He told the Commons what had happened – so far as he knew. He told them where the Government stood on the guarantee question. Wisely, he refrained from polemics until a great many more facts were known, and the Government had had proper opportunity to review its policy.

The Opposition exploded. David Grenfell, the official spokesman for the Labour Party, sneered 'that the Prime Minister is about the only person in diplomatic circles in Europe who can afford the splendid sense of isolation and detachment that he presented today . . .' Josiah Wedgwood, that turbulent critic – often so profoundly right, often so disastrously wrong – went much further: 'I believe that the Prime Minister at Munich, before Munich and since Munich, has been blinded by his affection for the dictators, that dictatorship is dearer to him than democracy . . .'

In the next few days, a good many facts became clear, and it became possible to draw certain conclusions from the new German aggression. For the first time, the lands affected were not German in population. Hitler had proved beyond argument or doubt that his territorial objectives in Europe were not limited to gathering all Germans within the Third Reich: indeed, it was difficult to see what limits, if any, existed to his long-term objectives. Every state lying to the east or south-east of Germany stood in obvious peril. Innumerable people who had felt a greater or lesser measure of sympathy with the German arguments against the 1919 settlement had doubtless decided that Germany must soon be resisted to the point of war.

These effects must have been clearly foreseeable to Hitler before he decided to order the march on Prague. Why, then, did he do it? Nobody could believe that any question of military defence was involved, for the Czechs were rapidly reducing their army, and showed every disposition to adopt whatever foreign policy the Germans might choose to demand. Some people talked of economic advantages which would accrue to Germany; but this argument was not very convincing, for a small landlocked state surrounded on three sides by the Reich and on the fourth by a German satellite could hardly resist any sort of economic pressure which Germany might care to exert. Only two explanations seemed credible: first, that Hitler proposed to enslave, expel or exterminate the Czechs to provide German *Lebensraum*; second (and on the whole more probable), that he coveted the military equipment of the Czech army so profoundly that it was worth all the disadvantages to go and seize it. The British Military Attaché in Berlin concluded that the bulk of war stocks and reserves of the Czecho-Slovak army were situated in Bohemia and Moravia, and would therefore fall into German hands. Hitherto, he argued, Germany had only been capable of arming a little over a hundred divisions, against a manpower potential little short of three hundred; the Czech armaments 'will increase her fighting power on land by probably much more than 25%'.[2] Even the *Daily Express*, which took an overtly isolationist line on foreign policy, was constrained to note that Hitler's plunder from the Czech lands included 'the Skoda works, the Bren arms factory. Millions of skilled workers. £60 millions of gold and foreign exchange. 1500 military aircraft.'[3] Evidently the Germans had many further designs; the acquisition of Bohemia and Moravia was a means, not an end.

On Saturday 18 March, just three days after the seizure of Prague, the British Cabinet was summoned to an emergency meeting. Tilea, the Romanian Minister in London, had told Halifax of a German ultimatum to his country, demanding economic hegemony. If this were conceded, Germany would secure such vast resources of oil and food that she would no longer be vulnerable to British naval blockade; indeed, there would be nothing to prevent her pushing her actual or effective frontiers to the Mediterranean. Before the Cabinet could meet, further news was received from the Romanian Minister of Foreign Affairs, which flatly contradicted his London representative's story of an 'ultimatum'. To compound the mystery, Tilea, when confronted with this denial, persisted in his statement.

True or false, the ultimatum story focused attention on a very serious potential threat, and gave the Cabinet opportunity to discuss the general orientation of its foreign policy. The Chiefs of Staff had no time to give a considered judgement on the military implications of a German attack on Romania, but their provisional view was that Britain and France alone could do nothing to prevent Romania being overrun; yet if Romania could be buttressed by Poland and Russia, then Britain and France would be in a position to intervene effectively in the west.

Chamberlain took the occasion of that Cabinet meeting to raise the widest possible questions of foreign policy. Events of the past week had resolved his personal uncertainties; as he told his colleagues:

Up till a week ago we had proceeded on the assumption that we should be able to continue with our policy of getting on to better terms with the Dictator Powers, and that although those Powers had aims, those aims were limited. We had all along had at the back of our minds the reservation that this might not prove to be the case but we had felt that it was right to try out the possibilities of this course . . .

He had now come definitely to the conclusion that Herr Hitler's attitude made it impossible to continue to negotiate on the old basis with the Nazi regime . . .

Chamberlain now turned and asked his Cabinet colleagues whether they concurred in a new policy which involved abandoning the whole idea of appeasement, deciding at what point a suitable stand could be made, and securing the widest possible alliance of Powers to join in making that stand. In fact the Prime Minister had made a speech in Birmingham the previous night in which he had already aired these ideas.

Chamberlain's colleagues concurred. Even Lord Maugham, who had been so hesitant during the September crisis, 'had reached the conclusion that we should probably have to fight Germany before very long'. Halifax saw the position as a sort of Morton's Fork: 'The attitude of the German Government was either bluff, in which case it would be stopped by a public declaration on our part; or it was not bluff, in which case it was necessary that we should all unite to meet it, and the sooner we united the better.' Views from the Dominions, as reported by Inskip (now Dominions Secretary) were broadly similar. There was some feeling in Canada that it was not appropriate to take a stand over Romania when no firm stand had been adopted over Czecho-Slovakia; yet even South Africa – always most pro-German of the Dominions – 'seemed likely to support us in resisting German aggression'. Ernest Brown assessed the most elusive and important factor of all: '. . . Public opinion had changed considerably in the past few days. Whereas in the autumn the detestation of war had perhaps counted for more than hatred of tyranny, he thought the position was now reversed.'

There can be little doubt that most people at all levels of society, and in all Parties, concurred in the general drift of these arguments. Where the stand should be made was a technical question for the diplomats and military men; what was not seriously in doubt was the proposition that a stand should be made, and made soon, that Germany should be told, in the most emphatic language, that any transgression of certain defined frontiers of Europe, on whatever pretext, would constitute an act of war against Britain, and against every possible ally whom Britain could rally to her side.

In the period between Munich and the march on Prague, the press as a whole had already moved a considerable way from appeasement. Opposition newspapers were a great deal more emphatic than they had been at the time of the September crisis. Some elements of the Conservative Press – of which the *Daily Telegraph* and the *Yorkshire Post* were most noteworthy – had come round to a position as strongly opposed to German designs as that of any Opposition newspaper. The *Telegraph* reacted clearly and immediately when German troops crossed the Czech frontier, without awaiting any sort of lead from the Government: 'Germany has perpetrated an affront to the whole civilised world which will not be readily forgotten'.[4] *The Times* was no less pungent the following day: 'No defence of any kind, no pretext of the slightest plausibility, can be offered for the violent extinction of Czech independence in the historic Czech homelands of Bohemia and Moravia.[5] Such words gain added force when we recall the support given by that same newspaper to Sudetendeutsch separatism six months earlier.

Other newspapers reacted at first in a very different manner. The *Daily Express* was indifferent: 'The destruction of Czechoslovakia cannot possibly be a matter of concern for Britain to the extent of leading us into any commitments on the Continent of Europe. These distant regions on the Danube lie quite outside our bailiwick. We cannot be expected to influence the course of events there.[6] First reactions of the *Daily Mail* came perilously near to jubilation:

> After an existence of twenty years, Czecho-Slovakia is dead. It has fallen into its component parts. The process is natural. The collapse was inevitable . . . There is nothing in this event either for alarm or fear. Rather should its disappearance be welcomed, for so long as it existed, whole or truncated, it was a danger to European peace. Another big mistake made at Versailles has been rectified. Europe should rejoice that more frontiers have changed without resort to a big conflict.[7]

Nor were such opinions confined to the political 'right'. Lord Arnold – formerly Sydney Arnold – once sat as a Liberal M.P. but had defected long since to the Labour Party. On 20 March he rhetorically asked the House of Lords:

> Did what had happened in the last week or ten days justify a real change of attitude? If war should come the case that would be put before the country was that Germany was out for world domination and that we must fight to defend our liberties. A case put in that way was going a long way in advance of anything which had yet happened.[8]

Thus Chamberlain faced some considerable difficulty in educating a section both of his own following and of the Opposition to the new policy he had outlined. The bulk of the Opposition, however, was willing enough to cooperate in a policy of military resistance to Germany. Labour was in no mood to attempt to strike down the Government: as Lloyd George's organiser, Colonel Tweed, wrote to his chief, 'It is interesting to note that even in Labour circles there is no suggestion that Attlee should be substituted for the obstinate third-rater who controls the present destiny of Britain'.[9]

Later in the month a delegation from Labour met Chamberlain, Wilson and Cadogan[10] – the last of these 'looking more like a dead fish than ever', commented Dalton.[11] The Prime Minister was very frank about the difficulties which he was currently encountering with potential allies in the east; while the general tone of the meeting appears to have delighted the delegates. Thus wrote Dalton:

> We all got the impression that the Prime Minister now realised that this 'appeasement' policy has been a failure, that he is completely disillusioned with Hitler, and very apprehensive about the future. The Government, or at least a majority in the Cabinet (Simon and others still dissenting) is now trying, though belatedly, to operate a collective security policy.[12]

Although there remained many problems both at home and abroad, the Cabinet committed itself to the practice as well as the theory of the new policy. On 18 March, they agreed 'that we should make approaches to Russia, Poland, Yugoslavia, Turkey, Greece and Romania with a view to obtaining assurances from them that they would join with us in resisting any sort of German aggression aimed at obtaining domination in South-Eastern Europe . . .'[13] This policy was rather drastically modified a couple of days later, when the Ministers decided to confine their approach to France, Poland and Russia, and to confine the initial agreement to one for 'consultations' between the four Powers. The spirit, however, was not altered, and it was universally accepted that the 'conversations' should serve as a prelude to action, not a substitute for action. The next major German encroachment must be resisted to the point of war. Chamberlain spelt out the new policy to his colleagues, very bluntly:

> The precise form which the *casus belli* might take was perhaps not very material. The real issue was that if Germany showed signs that she intended to proceed with her march for world domination, we must take steps to stop her by attacking her on two fronts. We should attack Germany, not in order to save a particular victim, but in order to put down the bully.[14]

The new policy was announced in only slightly muted language in the House of Commons the same afternoon. The *Daily Express* correctly judged the measure of the change:

> Perhaps the swiftest change of policy we have ever known occurred last week end within the sight of us all. It was the change from the policy of appeasement and rejection of Collective Security to the policy of abolishing appeasement and putting Collective Security in its place . . . The Prime Minister who was the leader of the policy of conciliation now becomes the leader of the policy of Collective Securtiy.[15]

Organs like the *Daily Herald* and the *New Chronicle* went as near as an Opposition newspaper can ever go in the direction of applauding the

Prime Minister and his new policy.

With impressive alacrity, those Government newspapers who had been more Chamberlainite than Chamberlain adjusted themselves to the change. On 15 March, the *Daily Mail* had written, 'The turmoil is purely local. Europe maintains calm.' Next day, the same newspaper recorded that M.P.s 'naturally saw cause for alarm'. The day after it asked a question which others – including Chamberlain and even Henderson – had asked long before: 'Is Herr Hitler indulging a Napoleonic vision of continental conquest? . . .' On 18 March, the *Mail* applauded the Prime Minister's Birmingham speech, which marked the first public break with appeasement: 'It held an unmistakable warning to the dictators that Britain stands firm.'

The *Daily Express* moved by a somewhat different route. The old 'isolationist' stance was not formally abandoned: Lord Arnold's speech was welcomed in the issue of 22 March. Although the newspaper was not convinced of the need to change its mind, it was prepared to set its views in cold storage, and use the new foreign policy of the Government to buttress another opinion which it had long held: 'The *Daily Express* is an isolationist newspaper. It adheres to that principle. But it is well aware of the argument for compulsory national service that is to be found in the present attempts to form a Grand Alliance.[16] Even people who believed that Britain and her Empire were the only things in the world worth defending must have felt some apprehension by this time that if Hitler secured mastery of Europe, it might prove inordinately difficult to defend the Empire and even the homeland against him.

Thus, within a week of the seizure of Prague, all organs of the national press, and all significant public figures, were united in the view that the Government should be allowed to go ahead and attempt to form its Grand Alliance.

Again arose the perennial problem of coordinating policies with the French. Initial reactions to the seizure of Prague were identical. Monsieur Bonnet, and the whole gamut of the French press, responded with the same indignation as the British, but also agreed that no immediate action was possible.[17] The two countries, everyone concurred, must stick together and intensify their rearmament.

About a week after the extinction of Czecho-Slovakia, conversations took place in London between Chamberlain and Halifax on the British side and Bonnet on the French, each flanked by ambassadors and diplomatic officials. The main discussion concerned the exceedingly difficult task of forging some kind of common defence between the Western Democracies and countries to the east which were menaced by Germany. The immediate danger to Romania had by no means evaporated, but people were already beginning to think of Poland as perhaps next on Hitler's list. Both Poland and Romania had acquired territory from Russia at the end of the war; both had good reason to fear that if Russian troops entered their country, whether as invaders or as ostensible allies, they would prove inordinately difficult to remove at a later date. The Poles would undoubtedly fight anyone who attacked them, and with virtual unanimity; yet they were acutely conscious that their national independence might well turn on maintaining some sort of balance between Germany and Russia, and not veering too far towards either. In Romania, the problem was somewhat different; as Bonnet pointed out, 'some of the upper classes preferred Hitler to Stalin.'[18] The British and French Ministers were anxious to bring Russia, Poland and Romania into alliance; but the reports they had received did not make them very sanguine about the prospects.

Conversations now turned to the more contentious question of the armaments of the Western Democracies. Chamberlain reminded Bonnet that in November Daladier had assured him that by the end of the spring France would be producing 400 aircraft a month. The French Foreign Minister was compelled to confess that in the past month the figure had been only 100 – though, by July or August, it would be about 250 or 300, and purchases were being made in the United States. Chamberlain recalled that in September the British aircraft production had been only 250 a month; currently, it stood around 580.

Bonnet replied with the inevitable French *tu quoque*. France, with forty million people, might be called upon to face Germany, with eighty millions, and Italy with forty millions. If Britain could not offer substantial help on land for, say, eighteen months, 'the consequences might be profound and irretrievable'. The position would be very different, however, if Britain was able to render substantial military assistance at the end of six or eight months. 'This led M. Bonnet to urge, with all the persuasion he could command, that this country should adopt in some form, whether direct conscription or otherwise, national service.' Not to put too fine a point on it, neither of the Western Democracies had great confidence in the will or capacity of the other to make an effective contribution to the common cause in event of war.

As if to underline the importance and urgency of agreement between the various threatened states, Germany took the very day of the Anglo-French discussions to seize the seaport of Memel from Lithuania. Ribbentrop had intimated to the Lithuanian Minister that if 'peaceful agreement' was not forthcoming, 'the German army would march in and would not stop at Memel'.[19]

The following day, Thursday 23 March, was the occasion of a State banquet at Buckingham Palace. Chamberlain gave his own account of the unexpected drama which accompanied the event. 'No sooner did I arrive than Hore-Belisha came up and whispered, "We have just got word that the Germans have mobilised twenty divisions on the western frontier. This is like the Brussels Ball."'[20] A day or two earlier, one may add, reports from Bucharest had spoken of German divisions massing on the Hungarian frontier.[21] These particular alarms and excursions proved without substance, and Europe experienced five months more of uneasy peace.

It soon became apparent that the 'Grand Alliance' policies on which the Western Powers had finally agreed were in any event futile. Chamberlain told the Cabinet Committee on Foreign Policy at its meeting of 27 March that 'any public association of Russia with the scheme would greatly diminish and weaken the authority of the common front'.[22] This feeling was very strong both in Poland and in Romania; other countries not immediately proposed for the alliance had made similar representations. Association with Russia would make potential allies 'extremely reluctant' to join; while conversely it would prove a good deal more difficult to suborn Italy and Japan from close association with Germany. The Poles made another point: if they were linked closely to Russia, this would be likely to precipitate a German attack on themselves.

Even at that meeting of 27 March, the prevailing view was that 'the country which on the whole seemed likely to be the next victim of German aggression' was Romania. The original idea of a four-Power alliance was virtually abandoned, when, almost by chance, the British Government turned to a new policy. On 29 March Chamberlain received a telephone call from Halifax, which led to a meeting between the two Ministers, Cadogan, and a journalist who had received impressive evidence

that Hitler had everything ready for a swoop on Poland which he had planned to split up between annexation and protectorate. This would be followed by absorption of Lithuania and then other states would be an easy prey. After that would come the possibility of a Russo-German alliance and finally the British Empire, the ultimate goal, would fall helplessly into the German maw.'[23]

Corroboratory evidence was received from elsewhere, and the Prime Minister became seriously alarmed 'that we might wake up on Sunday or Monday morning to find Poland surrendering to an ultimatum'. Chamberlain and Halifax 'then and there decided' that a guarantee must be issued to Poland to forestall such a move, and a Cabinet meeting was called for the following day. The Cabinet approved issue of the guarantee to Poland, which was announced in the House of Commons the day after, 31 March. Runciman, who was out of the country, was told that 'no attempt has been made to disguise the fact that this cover to Poland has been arranged to bridge the interval that must elapse before a regular form of agreement against aggression is worked out between the states involved'.[24] Nothing in politics is as permanent as a temporary expedient, and it was on the strength of her assurance to Poland – which was converted at the last moment into a formal alliance – that Britain eventually declared war on Germany.

Chamberlain had seen the Opposition leaders shortly before the Cabinet meeting of 30 March, and in the Parliamentary debate which followed the announcement there was not much controversy. Most saw the guarantee as an affirmation of the demand made by Labour's Arthur Greenwood – that 'an attack upon one [should be] an attack upon all' – as a step, in fact, towards the Grand Alliance. The one significant note of caution came from a rather unexpected quarter: Lloyd George. Russia, he declared, was 'the only country whose armies can get there . . . Unless the Poles are prepared to accept the only conditions with which we can successfully help them the responsibility must be theirs'. What, we may ask, was the moral if Poland thought that to invite Russian help was to incur certain destruction; or, alternatively, if Russia refused to proffer help? Politicians often spoke as if the guarantee to Poland was an act of British altruism; in fact the British Government's primary concern appears to have been to prevent Poland compounding with Germany.

Others shared Lloyd George's doubts. Runciman indicated privately that he was unhappy about an assurance to Poland which did not involve Russia.[25] Hankey thought that Lloyd Geroge's speech 'was exactly what ought to have been said, and I fear was not said, in Cabinet. The whole point is that *we* cannot save these eastern nations . . . We shall look terribly silly if Beck' – the Polish Foreign Minister – 'refuses to play with us, and sillier still if Hitler goes in and knocks Poland out and we fail to help.'[26] The matter had been considered in Cabinet more fully than these critics implied. Chatfield had told them at their meeting of 30 March that the Chiefs of Staff thought Poland would be overrun by Germany within two or three months; nevertheless, that Britain should declare war if the attack were made.

Very soon after Chamberlain's disillusionment with Hitler became complete, events drove him to very similar conclusions about Mussolini. Just after the extinction of Czecho-Slovakia, the Prime Minister wrote another personal note to the Duce, 'to convince him (1) that our quarrel was not with him but with Hitler (2) that if Hitler really intends to go on with these attempts to dominate the world a major war was inevitable and (3) that since he himself wanted peace it was up to him to bestir himself to get it.'[27] Mussolini's eventual reply 'was of such a formal kind and was wrapped in such a cloud of meaningless words that it was not possible to arrive at any conclusions about it.'[28] Shortly afterwards, however, the Italians occupied Albania. There was a slender argument available that this move was designed to forestall Hitler in the Balkans, but it did not carry much conviction. 'I am afraid,' wrote Chamberlain, 'that such faith as I ever had in the assurances of dictators is rapidly being whittled away'.[29]

Others who had joined in the Prime Minister's will to peace, though perhaps not in his original optimism, now joined in his despair. 'Right up to the last,' wrote Runciman, 'I have been anxious to support your efforts for peace, but it seems to me – so I interpret your recent telegram – that nothing effective can be done now.'[30]

On the assumption that war was inevitable – or at least highly probable – in the near future, a number of changes became necessary at home. For several months, the proposal had been bruited that a Ministry of Supply should be set up to secure material equipment for the armed forces. Sir Horace Wilson discussed the matter with industrialists two or three weeks after Munich. 'So far as they are aware,' he wrote, 'there has as yet been no failure on the part of industry to provide the supplies required by the Departments, except insofar . . . as there has been lack of the necessary equipment or the necessary very highly skilled labour.'[31] The case had evidently not been made for the innovation, and the Cabinet turned it down. The Ministry of Supply question, however, began to acquire some symbolic significance with the Opposition, who saw the Government's refusal as evidence of lack of determination to mobilise the national economy against aggression. The proposal was raised again, and more sympathetically, by Inskip in February 1939. He drew attention to the 'steadying' effect which it would have on public opinion. Even though the Ministry would have little function in peacetime, the operation of bringing it into existence in war would involve considerable initial difficulties.[32] Other Ministers still demurred; but after the events of March war became so highly probable that opposition melted away. Chatfield, who had been the most implacable Ministerial opponent, swung round in favour[33] and thereafter no one seriously fought the proposal. The Government decision in favour was eventually announced on 18 April, and the necessary legislation enacted in July.

Far more difficult was the question of military conscription. In an almost casual aside on the Ministry of Supply question, written in February, Inskip had commented: 'So far as I know, nobody has proposed that even in war against a major Power we should use land forces in any way comparable to those which we succeeded in deploying in the last war.'[34] How significant any conscript armies Britain could raise would prove in the event of war was dubious; but the diplomatic importance of conscription as a device for convincing France that Britain was ready to make real sacrifices of blood could not be overstated. A number of indivduals – mostly well to the political right – had long been agitating for conscription; but the Cabinet was by no means enamoured either of the proposal or of the growing insistence which the French set upon it. A report sent to Runciman on 3 April describes the Cabinet's last stand against conscription, at the meeting of 31 March:

> The Cabinet had decided that morning that the best answer to the cry for compulsory service was to increase the present establishment of the Territorial Army by the equivalent of two Divisions (40,000 men) and then to double it. The result has been undoubtedly to put an end to the cry for conscription, at any rate for the present . . . Criticism, if still

heard, is very largely hushed. Even the French, though not satisfied, are at any rate mollified and encouraged.[35]

The pressure, however, did not abate for long. At the Cabinet meeting of 19 April, Hore-Belisha reported 'more and more and more pressure from France and other countries abroad'.

Chamberlain had his private agonies on the matter. 'His own personal view', he told the Cabinet on 29 March, 'was favourable to [conscription]'. However, Baldwin, his predecessor, had promised not to introduce compulsory military service in peacetime during the lifetime of the current Parliament. That promise engaged Chamberlain too. The Prime Minister took refuge in a somewhat casuistic argument: '. . . that, although we were not actually at war, the state of affairs in which we now lived could not be described as peacetime in the ordinary meaning of the word.'[36]

Another even more serious difficulty attended any attempt to introduce compulsory military service: the likely effect it would have on Labour, in both political and industrial senses of the word. Labour, for some time, had been 'acting very helpfully and was turning a blind eye to a number of practices to which they would ordinarily raise objections. All this facilitated the rapid increase in the output of munitions.'[37] Some serious risk existed that any decision in favour of conscription would vitiate that cooperation, and the overall military effect might be worse than if the attempt had not been made.

Late in April, the Cabinet resolved to take the bull by the horns. On 27 April a motion in favour of compulsory military service was set before the House of Commons. Labour put up a formal, but perhaps perfunctory, opposition. The Liberals were split from top to bottom: six voting with the Government, and seven against it. Inevitably, the Government had its way; and the industrial trouble which had been feared did not materialise. It seems fair to conclude that many guessed at the international pressures which had forced the Government's hand; while even those who thought that the decision was unwise had already decided that war was so probable in the near future that any outright attack on measures which the Government might take in anticipation could prove infinitely damaging to the national interest.

The only really formidable opposition to conscription came from Northern Ireland. More than a month before the seizure of Prague, the Northern Ireland Cabinet endorsed the view of its Acting Prime Minister: '. . . having regard to the attitude of a certain section of the minority in Northern Ireland it would be practically impossible' to apply conscription there.[38] The same view was reaffirmed when the question of National Registration was raised in Great Britain.[39]

Thus did Britain face the advent of war in an atmosphere of gloomy resignation to the inevitable. The ostensible purpose of such a war had long been forgotten. It was difficult to envisage any circumstances in which the Western Allies could do much more than stand on the defensive, and perhaps pin down a significant number of Germans who would otherwise be fighting in the east. The Allies would fight in despair rather than hope; as the British Military Attaché in Berlin decided by April 1939, 'we must go to war now or never.'[40] A French diplomat had already invented a very descriptive phrase for the struggle which would soon take place: 'the war of the French and British succession'.[41]

How far people saw the inevitable logic of the situation in the middle or late spring of 1939 is difficult to say. They were probably reconciled to the inevitability of war, although – right to the last moment – a few incorrigible optimists, such as the *Daily Express* and the Sunday paper astrologers, proclaimed the opposite. The British people probably feared more destruction from the air, and more losses in the field, than they would eventually sustain. It is unlikely that they envisaged the fall of France in 1940, or that Britain would rapidly pass into the second rank of world powers, and her Empire fall to pieces in the aftermath of victory. 'Hawks' like Churchill apparently based their clamorous advice on a profound over-estimate of the remaining strength of the Western Democracies; but in their misjudgement they were very close to the mind of the British man in the street, in all classes and in all Parties. Just as no British Government could have led a united country into war over the Sudetenland in 1938, so also could no British Government have resisted the almost universal pressures which led to war in 1939.

It is always a source of argument in what particular considerations that popular feeling had its deepest roots. There were matters of national interest which motivated men like Chatfield, and which had substantial appeal to the man in the street in a cruder form. He did not pretend to understand the disposition of world forces, or the likely consequences of engagements with various world powers; but he could see with considerable clarity that if the various states menaced by Germany did not somehow stick together, Hitler would be able to gobble them up one by one. No doubt there were other even cruder feelings: for example, resentment that Germany, the defeated enemy of 1918, should dare to rise again and challenge Britain. But it would be wrong and unhistorical to see this rising spirit of national determination in terms of a mere calculation of interest. There were strong and growing moral considerations at work in Britain: pity for the various victims of Nazism; anger at the brutality and inhumanity of the Nazi system; a feeling that we were in the presence of a monster of pure evil which must – at whatever cost – be destroyed.

12 Analysis

'. . . Free Trade? What is it? Why, breaking down the barriers that separate nations; those barriers behind which nestle the feelings of pride, revenge, hatred and jealousy, which every now and then burst their bounds and deluge whole countries with blood, those feelings which nourish the poison of war and conquest . . .' Richard Cobden, 28 September 1843

The British Government which was in office during the 'year of Munich' has come under bitter attack from those who argued that unnecessary and dangerous concessions were made to the 'dictators'; it has also been stoutly defended by those who have argued that its wisdom bought eleven vital months for Britain to rearm. Before judgement on either score is attempted, it is fair to ask what real choice, if any, statesmen of the time had in the actual situations with which they were confronted. The year saw three great international changes: the Austrian *Anschluss*, the Munich settlement, and the final destruction of Czechoslovakia. Not even the most bitter critics of the governments of the Western Democracies have seriously suggested that there was any action which they could have taken either in March 1938 or in March 1939 which would radically have altered the course of events; but many have suggested that the British and French Governments handled the September crisis wrongly. The burden of this criticism is that – instead of acceding to transfer of the Sudetenland – Britain, France, Russia and Czechoslovakia should have told Hitler that any transgression of the existing frontiers of Czechoslovakia would entail instant war with all four.

As Sir Eric Phipps pointed out in the course of the crisis, one could not bluff Hitler. No threat of war would have had the slightest effect unless Hitler was convinced that the four Powers were both willing to fight a war against him, and capable of winning that war. The military evidence available to Britain suggested that they were in no position to win such a war, save perhaps at the end of a very long and exhausting struggle. This applied even if Germany fought alone, without allies.

The argument set against Munich, however, is not usually posited on the grounds that a war in 1938 would have resulted in an easy victory for the Allies, but on the grounds that a firm stand would have averted war altogether, by compelling Hitler to back down. Whether Hitler would have backed down in September 1938 appears highly doubtful; yet, as

Chamberlain pointed out to his colleagues, the confrontation of the previous May, which resulted in an apparent victory for Czechoslovakia against German pretensions, did not prove the end of the story. Even if Hitler had conceded defeat in September, there is every reason for believing that he would have simply bided his time until he felt stronger. Dictators, who control the organs of propaganda, are in a much more comfortable position in this respect than governments of parliamentary democracies, who usually find it difficult to maintain a high and expensive level of war preparation for very long. It was also reasonably certain that the four ill-assorted allies would have fallen out over something or other before long, which would have given Hitler his opportunity.

It is sometimes contended that a clear rebuff to Hitler would have precipitated internal revolution in Germany, and thus permanently removed the threat of Nazi aggression. To this one can best reply that the Germans most opposed to Hitler were, on the whole, of the older and wealthier classes; and such people do not usually make revolutions.

Whether or not we accept the view that Chamberlain's handling of the September crisis was the best possible way of dealing with the situation, there can surely be little dispute today that he acted both honourably and with reasonable regard to the evidence available to him. How, then, did he acquire the reputation of a foolish and gullible old man, or even a wilful traitor to whom dictatorship was dearer than democracy?

The most powerful arguments against Chamberlain do not really turn on the wisdom or unwisdom of the substantive measures which he took, but rather on the repeated indications that he believed Hitler to be speaking the truth. His declaration after Munich that he believed he had secured 'peace in our time', and the profound trust which he evidently placed in the declaration he made along with Hitler just after the main Munich conference, are two famous indications of that state of mind; and we have already seen that he spoke in similar vein to his Cabinet colleagues. Yet we must remember that several members of the Cabinet who did not share the Prime Minister's trust in Hitler nevertheless acknowledged the need to reach the Munich settlement. Conversely, statesmen of other countries, like Beck and Stalin, sometimes reposed considerable confidence in Hitler – with even more disastrous results for their countries. Indeed, Chamberlain's confidence in Hitler was never complete, and his recommendation of the settlement seems to carry the overtone, 'At best this will do much good; at worst it will still, on balance, do more good than harm'. The Prime Minister would scarcely have improved prospects for the future if he had risen in the House of Commons and spoken in terms like these:

> There is an outside chance that Hitler may be speaking the truth, though many in the Cabinet do not trust a word he says. We all, however, perceive that he has got us at an extreme disadvantage, and

most of us agree with the view of our military men that if war must come it is better to delay for six months or so, and meanwhile push ahead with our rearmament.

The Opposition was also incapable of making many of the best points against the Government. They dared not say in so many words that it would have been better to go to war (or at least incur a great risk of war) than cede the Sudetenland. They could hardly deplore the country's military weakness when their own support for rearmament was so recent and so far from unanimous. They were certainly in no position to criticise the Government's failure to employ Mussolini as a counterpoise to Hitler, for they had bitterly attacked all efforts towards an Anglo-Italian *rapprochement*, and until well on in 1938 showed every sign of believing Italy to be the greater enemy.

As Chamberlain's Government incurred such intense criticism in later times for the decisions it took in September 1938, it is surprising that the decisions which it took in March and April 1939, which were in every sense less responsible and less rational, have attracted so much less criticism. In the spring of 1938, the Government decided that it would be useless and counter-productive to attempt to form a 'Grand Alliance'. All the arguments available in 1938 were still available a year later; yet the Government went ahead and made the attempt, with results exactly as they had themselves predicted earlier. They then proceeded to guarantee Poland, even though they realised Poland could not be saved from destruction. The great majority of the Government's critics likewise did not seem very interested as to whether anything could actually be done to help the Poles. ~~but this wasn't the point as Cham [illegible]~~

The question is often raised: 'Why did Britain go to war over Poland in 1939, when she had refused to go to war over Czechoslovakia in 1938?' The short answer is that the decisions of 1938 were taken largely on military calculations, partly on the chance that Hitler might mean what he said, and partly because it would be exceedingly difficult to explain to world opinion, to Dominion opinion and even to home opinion why it was worth fighting a great war in order to prevent the Sudetendeutsch joining Germany. The decision of 1939, however, was taken by men pushed to the point of desperation, who felt that if a stand was not made over Poland, whatever the military prospects, it would never be possible to make a stand anywhere.

If we are led to the view that the settlement of September 1938 was probably wise and certainly rational, then at what point (if any) did Britain 'go wrong'?

Munich was a natural corollary of the Austrian *Anschluss*. The only possible way of preventing the *Anschluss* lay in getting on terms with Mussolini. When Chamberlain wrote to him in July 1937, it was in all probability too late to restore the Stresa Front; but there was a slender chance that a rapid agreement might have given Mussolini both the will and the capacity to resist Hitler. Mussolini would assuredly have extracted his price: recognition of Italy's position in Abyssinia, British disinterest in the Spanish Civil War. There was risk that such a policy would have involved a fatal breach with France, and without doubt all the high-minded critics would have exploded in wrath at the Government; but the sombre fact remains that this was the one slender chance to hold back Germany from her career of conquest without war which presented itself after Chamberlain had assumed the Premiership. Chamberlain's fault was not — as most critics have suggested — that he intruded in foreign policy, but that he allowed his first Foreign Secretary to have his head for much too long.

Criticism of Chamberlain's foreign policy is often posited on the grounds that the whole idea of 'appeasement' towards the 'dictators' was wrong from the outset. Part of the trouble here, as we have already seen, stems from confusion as to what the word 'appeasement' meant, at least before 1938, to the people who used it. Some critics, however, seem to have taken the much more radical view that the whole idea of securing some kind of *détente* with 'dictators' was wrong *ab initio*.

It is perhaps pertinent to ask who were the 'dictators'. If by the word 'dictator' we mean a person in whose hands a very large degree of executive power is concentrated, then in 1938 most states in Europe were dictatorships, and every one of the European states which proponents of the 'Grand Alliance' sought to link with Britain and France in defence of Czechoslovakia was undeniably a dictatorship. The 'dictators', however, were usually taken to mean Hitler and Mussolini, with perhaps Franco added. This view is really an extraordinary one; for, beyond doubt, Stalin in particular possessed a far greater concentration of executive power than Mussolini or even Hitler. His record of treatment of political opponents before 1938 was incomparably more vicious than that of any man in the world. It is sometimes forgotten that the worst horrors of Hitler's régime belong to the wartime period. The one aspect in which Stalin appeared objectively preferable to Hitler or Mussolini was that he showed little disposition to attack contiguous states; though whether this useful characteristic was founded in lack of will or in lack of power was a matter of speculation at the time, and the answer is today known all too well. Many people seem to have had a curious set of double standards when they discussed the race of 'dictators'.

Unless we subscribe to these double standards, it is difficult to escape the conclusion that the policy of 'appeasement' in the original sense was about the most sensible course to follow in the world which Chamberlain found when he took office in 1937. The balance of forces was changing very rapidly, and the post-war political settlement was bound to be challenged. As that challenge was inevitable, then surely it was better that the changes should be brought about peacefully through negotiations, rather than by war or blatant threat of war? If Hitler and Mussolini were in a position to enforce change, then it was wiser to negotiate with them than to await passively the course of events.

If, then, we conclude that Chamberlain made the best of an extremely bad international situation down to mid-March 1938, then the place or places where the fundamental errors were made must be sought in the period before Chamberlain became Prime Minister.

Various dates in the 1930s have been suggested as the turning point, as the last moment when it was possible to halt the course of events which would lead to world war. These dates include the German military occupation of the Rhineland in March 1936; the Italian invasion of Abyssinia in October 1935; the Japanese attack on China which commenced in September 1931. At all of these points, however, the question is the same: Did it lie in the power of a British Government to compel the aggressor to withdraw? It is difficult to see how in any of these cases the answer could be other than negative. Whether Britain was physically in a position to come to grips with the offenders seems doubtful; whether the British people would have countenanced policies which risked war on any of these occasions is even more so. As the Abyssinian episode showed, economic measures were not merely ineffective, they were disastrously counter-productive.

It is not difficult to pick out other occasions in the early 1930s, or in the 1920s, when decisions taken by British politicians increased the danger of war. The firm impression remains, however, that even if that particular war with that particular enemy had been averted, some other major European war would probably have come. The crucial decisions seem to be those taken immediately after the First World War – though for reasons different from those which many critics of 'Versailles' have suggested.

In the spring of 1938, when British statesmen were compelled to consider the Sudetenland question as a matter of urgency, they were reminded that the decision to include the territory within Czechoslovakia was originally taken partly for economic reasons: in order to balance the mainly agricultural Slav regions with a predominantly industrial area. Why, we may ask, was this considered necessary? Why should the Great Powers, or the Czechs themselves, have wished to incorporate a substantial number of people with a very different language and culture from the majority, when these people could have been included relatively easily in Germany or Austria? There were similar questions in other future trouble-spots. There was not the slightest doubt that Danzig was German. Why, then, should the Poles have been anxious that it should become and remain a Free City under the League of Nations, while the Germans were anxious that it should return to the Reich? Why was Memel – also undeniably German – first created a Free City, and later seized by Lithuania?

The answers to all these questions are similar. One of the most fundamental assumptions made by European states in 1919 and thereafter was economic nationalism: the idea that the nation-state should form, so far as possible, a self-contained economic unit, surrounded by tariffs, quotas and other barriers to trade with outsiders. It was important for the Czechs to possess the Sudetenland not only because it was part of historic Bohemia, but also because the Sudetendeutsch would consume the agricultural surplus of Slav peasants, who would encounter difficulties if they attempted to sell across national boundaries. It was also important to the Czechs that the industrial products which they needed could be obtained from within their own economic unit, lest they should be at the mercy of hostile economic policies pursued by foreign governments. It was important to Poland that Danzig should not be German, because it would then be possible for the Germans to impede or tax Polish trade which – until Gdynia was built – had no other convenient channel to the outside world. For similar reasons, it was important for Lithuania to control Memel.

Thus the fundamental weakness of the 1919 settlement was that it failed to tackle the question of economic nationalism: indeed, it made matters even worse than they had been before 1914. In place of the three great Empires of Central and Eastern Europe, the peacemakers set up, or ratified, a mass of states, each determined so far as it could to become economically self-sufficient. Behind the trade barriers erected by those states there grew pressure-groups of capital or labour or both combined, who spoke of 'trade wars', or 'exporting unemployment', and demanded more trade barriers still. In the end, Germany (and others too) came to dream of wars of conquest, to establish a hegemony over neighbours which would give captive markets to their exporters, and ensure that their own nationals did not suffer from adverse trade policies pursued by outsiders. Britain, the last great Free Trade nation, abandoned her traditional policy piecemeal during the inter-war period, making the final break in 1932 with the general imposition of tariffs. This served as a most baleful example to others. Neville Chamberlain, the 'Appeasement' Prime Minister of 1938, was attempting to cope with a political situation which was to a large extent the fault of Neville Chamberlain, the 'Protectionist' Chancellor of the Exchequer of 1932.

Although the situation which Chamberlain tried to meet in 1938 had causes which were largely economic, it was no longer possible by that time to administer an economic cure – or, indeed, any cure at all. Too many interests, too many emotions, had been engaged on all sides. We have already had cause to note how in 1938 many of the older and wealthier Germans felt the gravest apprehensions about political expansion which carried the risk of war; but their counsels had been swept aside by others who were stirred by emotions which were largely non-economic in character.

This argument, in its most extreme form, could lead us not merely to the view that there was no chance of saving peace in 1938, but to the conclusion that the 1919 'settlement', or the economic policies of the very early 1930s, would have led to the Second World War, even if Hitler, Mussolini and Stalin had all never lived. There may be a germ of truth in that; but the present author contends for a milder proposition. The policies of economic nationalism sowed the dragon's teeth; but it was not certain that they would germinate and the armed men spring forth. As the years advanced, the danger increased, and the measure of statesmanship required to avert that war also increased. By 1938 – probably several years before – the prospect of preserving peace was negligibly small. Neville Chamberlain failed because he attempted the impossible; but it does him no dishonour that he made the attempt.

Notes

1 PRELUDE

1 Notes by the First Sea Lord . . . 5 January 1937, sent to FLA 22 July. CHT/3/ fo. 193 seq.
2 Cabinet 35 (37), 29 September. CAB 23/89.
3 Cabinet 37 (37), 13 October. CAB 23/89.
4 Dalton diary, 11 April 1938.
5 Sinclair to Lord Allen, 22 March 1938 (copy). THRS 2/38/1.
6 Sir Eric Phipps to Eden, 30 September 1937 (copy). PHPP 1/19 fo. 11.
7 Cabinet 3 (38), 2 February. CAB 23/92.
8 Eden to Chamberlain, 9 January 1938. PREM 1/276.
9 Earl of Avon, *Facing the Dictators* (London, 1962) p. 324.
10 Hankey to Phipps, 21 February 1938. PHPP 3/3 fo. 81.
11 F.O. minute, 29 July 1937. FO 371/21160.
12 Cabinet 34 (37), 6 September. CAB 23/89.
13 Chamberlain to Mussolini, 27 July 1937 (copy). PREM 1/276.
14 F.O. telegram, 4 August 1937. PREM 1/276.
15 Chamberlain – Halifax – Vansittart correspondence, 3–5 August 1937. PREM 1/276.
16 Halifax to Chamberlain, 19 August 1937. PREM 1/275.
17 Eden to Ingram (draft), 8 September 1937. FO 371/21161.
18 Note by Vansittart towards telegram to Perth, 1 October 1937. FO 371/21162 fo. 10.
19 Notes by Ingram, Sargent, Vansittart, 11–12 November 1937. FO 371/21162, fo. 188 seq.
20 Ibid.
21 Perth to Cadogan, 23 December 1937. FO 371/22402 fo. 58 seq.
22 Cabinet 43 (37), 24 November. CAB 23/9/A.
23 Printed Cabinet paper by Vansittart, December 1937. VNST 1/21.
24 Hankey to Phipps, 11 January 1938. PHPP 3/3 fo. 75 seq.
25 Ibid., fo. 79.
26 Dalton diary, 12 April 1938.
27 Ibid., 4 November 1937.
28 Neville to Hilda Chamberlain, 5 December 1937. NC 18/1/1031.
29 Eden to Chamberlain, 1 January 1938. PREM 1/276.
30 Ibid., 31 January 1938. PREM 1/276.
31 Cranborne to Eden, 4 February 1938. PREM 1/276.
32 Neville to Hilda Chamberlain, 13 March 1938. NC 18/1/1041.
33 Perth to Cadogan, 6 February 1938. PREM 1/276.
34 Eden – Chamberlain letters, 8 February 1938. PREM 1/276.
35 Cabinet 8 (38), 19 February. CAB 23/92.
36 Hankey to Phipps, 21 February 1938. PHPP 3/3 fo. 81.
37 Ibid.
38 Ibid.
39 Perth to Eden, 17 February 1938. FO 371/22403 fo. 156
40 Perth to Eden, 16 February 1938. PREM 1/276.
41 Perth to F.O., 17 February 1938. PREM 1/276.

42 E. M. B. Ingram to Perth (draft), 21 February 1938. PREM 1/276.
43 Hankey to Phipps, 21 February 1938. PHPP 3/3 fo. 81.
44 Record of events . . . (Halifax). N. D. Templewood X. 3.
45 Cabinet 6 (38), 19 February 1938. CAB 23/92.
46 Record of events . . . (Halifax). N. D. Templewood X. 3.
47 Ibid.
48 See Chamberlain – Eden correspondence, January – February 1938, PREM 1/276; also
Earl of Avon, *Facing the Dictators*, pp. 555–9.
49 Crewe to J. A. Spender (copy), 28 February 1938. Crewe C/46.
50 *Liberal Magazine*, 1938, pp. 97–8.

2 THE FLOOD GATES OPEN

1 R. Bernays, H. Crookshank to Chamberlain, 23 February 1938. NC 17/11/32/92, 14.
2 Cabinet 6 (38), 19 February. CAB 23/92.
3 Cabinet 10 (38), 2 March. CAB 23/92.
4 Henderson to Halifax, 10 March 1938. *Documents in British Foreign Policy 1919–1939*, 3rd
Series, vol. 1. DBFP 1 No. 4.
5 Cabinet 12 (38), 12 March. CAB 23/92.
6 Ibid.
7 Halifax to Henderson, 12 March 1938. DBFP 1 No. 54; but see also Henderson to
Halifax, 16 March. FO 800/313 fo. 35 seq.
8 Henderson to Halifax, 16 March 1938 (copy). FO 800/269 fo. 50 seq.
9 W. Ward Price memorandum, 23 March 1938. FO 800/313 fo. 54 seq.
10 Neville to Hilda Chamberlain, 13 March 1938. NC 18/1/1041.
11 Jan Masaryk to Halifax, 12 March 1938. DBFP 1 No. 63.
12 Printed Cabinet memorandum, 21 March 1938. VNST 1/23.
13 Henderson to Halifax, 1 April 1938. DBFP 1 No. 121.
14 Appreciation of the situation in the event of war against Germany in 1939 . . ., 26
October 1936. C.O.S. 513 (J.P.) CAB 53/29.
15 Neville to Ida Chamberlain, 20 March 1938. NC 18/1/1042.
16 Chilston to Halifax, enc., 19 April 1938. DBFP 1 No. 148.
17 Advisory Committee . . ., April 1938. LPEC Vol. 76 p. 713.
18 Chilston to Halifax, 17 March 1938. DBFP 1 No. 92.
19 R. C. W. Firebrace to Chilston, 18 April 1938. DBFP 1 No. 151.
20 See, e.g., Runciman to Chamberlain, 21 September 1938. Correspondence respecting
Czechoslovakia September 1938. Cmd. 5847.
21 Dalton diary, 24 June 1937.
22 Newton to Halifax, 1 November 1938. FO 371/21580 fo. 161 seq.
23 Palairet to Halifax, 14 March 1938. DBFP 1 No. 76.
24 Pares to Newton, 19 March 1938. DBFP 1 No. 97.
25 Phipps to Halifax, 15 March 1938. DBFP 1 No. 81.
26 Hankey to James, 15 March 1938. CAB 21/585.
27 Unsigned document, 15 March 1938. CAB 21/585.
28 Phipps to Halifax, 18, 27 March 1938 (copy). PHPP 1/20, fos 1, 13.
29 Halifax to Chamberlain, 19 March 1938. PREM 1/265 fo. 309.
30 Military implications of German aggression against Czechoslovakia. C.O.S. 697 (J.P.)
CAB 53/37 fo. 105 seq. The printed version is dated 28 March 1938, but a form of the
document was in the hands of the Cabinet for their meeting of 22 March.
31 F.P. (36), 26th meeting, 18 March 1938. CAB 23/623.
32 Dalton diary, 8 April 1938.
33 Cadogan to Henderson, 22 April 1938. FO 800/269 fo. 103 seq.
34 F.P. (36) 26th meeting, 18 March 1938. CAB 27/623.
35 Neville to Ida Chamberlain, 20 March 1938. NC 18/1/1042.

36 Cabinet 15 (38) 22 March. CAB 23/93.

3 HOPES AND FEARS

1 Neville to Hilda Chamberlain, 27 March 1938. NC 18/1/1043.
2 F.P. (36) 26th meeting, 18 March 1938. CAB 27/623.
3 Ibid.
4 Phipps to Halifax, 11 April 1938. FO 800/311, fos 27–8.
5 Halifax to Phipps, 13 April 1938 (copy). FO 800/311 fo. 30.
6 E. Beneš, *Memoirs* (London, 1954) p. 39.
7 Halifax to Phipps, 11 April 1938. DBFP 1 No. 135.
8 Cadogan to Halifax, 20 April 1938. FO 800/313 fo. 96 seq.
9 Pares to Newton, enc. in Newton to Halifax, 6 April 1938. DBFP 1 No. 130.
10 Newton to Halifax, 4 May 1938. DBFP 1 No. 176.
11 Henderson to Halifax, 3 May 1938. DBFP 1 No. 167.
12 Hoare to Halifax, 25 March 1938 (copy). Templewood X. 3.
13 Halifax to Chamberlain, 9 May 1938; Chamberlain to Vansittart 10 May (copy). PREM 1/265 fos 286 ff., 284.
14 Churchill to Chamberlain, 15 May 1938. PREM 1/249, fo. 124 seq.
15 Henderson to S. M. Bruce, 25 May 1937 (copy). FO 800/268 fo. 220 seq.
16 Cabinet 22 (38), 4 May. CAB 23/95.
17 Henderson to Halifax, 22 August 1938. DBFP 2 No. 665.
18 Seton-Watson/Hoare correspondence, 22–5 March 1938. Templewood X. 3.
19 Newton to Halifax, 19 April 1938. DBFP 1 No. 149.
20 Dep. Julius Stano to Runciman, 31 August 1938. FO 800/305 fo. 463 seq.
21 C.I.D., C.O.S., 245th meeting, 25 July 1938. CAB 53/9.
22 Halifax to Phipps, 11 April 1938. DBFP 1 No. 135.
23 Halifax to Newton, 2 May 1938. DBFP 1 No. 166.
24 Neville to Ida Chamberlain, 1 May 1938. NC 18/1/1049.
25 Ibid., 13 May 1938. NC 18/1/1051.
26 Newton to Halifax, 17 May 1938. DBFP 1 No.
27 Cabinet 25 (38), 22 May. CAB 23/93.
28 Halifax to Henderson (telegram), 22 May 1938, appendix to ibid.
29 Neville to Ida Chamberlain, 28 May 1938. NC 1/18/1054.
30 Ibid.
31 Henderson to Halifax, 6 March 1939, encl. (copy). CAB 21/540.
32 Ibid., 18 February 1939 (copy). FO 800/270 fo. 10 seq.
33 Report of Lt-Col. Strange. DBFP 1 No. 365.
34 Halifax to Newton, 4 June 1938. DBFP 1 No. 374.
35 Halifax to Dawson, 15 June 1938 (copy). FO 800/309 fo. 183 seq.
36 Dawson to Halifax, 19 June 1938. FO 800/309 fo. 186 seq.
37 Newton to Halifax, 2 June, 16 July, 2 August 1938. DBFP1 Nos 368, 496; DBFP 2 No. 567.
38 Halifax to Newton, 22 June 1938. DBFP 1 No. 432.
39 F.P. (36) 31st meeting, 16 June 1938. CAB 27/624.
40 Wilson to Halifax, 22 June, with pencilled note (Halifax). PREM 1/265 fos 232–4.
41 Runciman to Halifax, 30 June 1938 (copy). WR 292.
42 Runciman–Chamberlain correspondence, 7–10 May 1937. NC 7/11/30/112, 113.
43 Wilson to Halifax, 22 June 1938. FO 800/309 fo. 194 seq.
44 Halifax to Runciman, 1 July 1938. W.R. 292.
45 See, for example, Runciman correspondence, FO 800/309 fos 201–8.
46 Halifax to Runciman, 15 July 1938. W.R. 292.
47 Halifax to Newton, 16 July 1938. DBFP 1 No. 493.
48 Newton to Halifax, 20 July 1938. FO 371/21728.

49 F.O. minutes 18, 28 July 1938. FO 371/21729.
50 Von Ribbentrop to Halifax, 21 August 1938 (copy). PREM 1/265 fos 206–9.
51 *Evening Standard*, 26 July 1938.
52 *News Chronicle*, 27 July 1938.
53 Runciman to Chamberlain, 1 August 1938. NC 7/11/31/231.
54 Runciman to Halifax, (?) 4 August 1938 (copy). WR 296.
55 Runciman to Halifax, 10 August 1938. DBFP 2 No. 602.
56 Halifax to Runciman, 18 August 1938. DBFP 2 No. 643.
57 Cabinet 32 (38), 13 July. CAB 23/94.
58 Minute on German political situation, 9 August 1938. VNST 2/36. Henderson to Newton, 11 August 1938 (copy). FO 800/309 fo. 219 seq.
59 Meeting of Ministers, 30 August 1938. CAB 23/94.
60 Henderson to Halifax (telegram), 25 August 1938. FO 800/309 fo. 265 seq.
61 Minute to the above, 27 August 1938.
62 Sargent minute, 12 August 1938. FO 800/314 fo. 47.
63 Wilson to Chamberlain, 25 August 1938. PREM 1/265 fos 194–8.
64 Ashton-Gwatkin to Strang, 29 August 1938. FO 800/304 fo. 213 seq.
65 Stopford memorandum, 26 August 1938. FO 800/304 fos 223–3.
66 Minute of conversation between Stopford and Smutny, 1 September 1938. FO 800/304 fo. 131.
67 Runciman to Halifax, 5 September 1938. DBFP 2 No. 783.
68 Cabinet 37 (38), 12 September. CAB 23/95.
69 Boothby to Chamberlain, 27 July 1938 (copy). FO 371/21730.

4 MOMENT OF TRUTH

1 *News Chronicle*, 29 August 1938.
2 Vansittart to Halifax, 31 August 1938. FO 800/314 fo. 98 seq.
3 Neville to Ida Chamberlain, 3 September 1938. NC 18/1/1066.
4 Chamberlain to Halifax, 30 August 1938 (copy). PREM 1/265 fos 180–1.
5 Meeting of Ministers, 30 August 1938. CAB 23/94.
6 Inskip diary, 8 September 1938. INKP 1.
7 Vansittart memorandum, 7 September 1938. VNST 2/39.
8 Neville to Hilda Chamberlain, 6 September 1938. NC 18/1/1067.
9 Samuel note, 16 September 1938. Samuel A/118 fos 1–4. For other reactions see Cabinet 37 (38), 12 September, CAB 23/93; Newton, Phipps and Masaryk to Halifax, all 7 September, FO 371/21764; Halifax to Chilston, 8 September, DBFP 2 No. 808.
10 Samuel note, 16 September 1938. Samuel A/118 fos 1–4.
11 *Daily Telegraph*; *News Chronicle*, 9 September 1938.
12 Cabinet 37 (38), 13 September. CAB 23/95.
13 Ibid., 12 September. CAB 23/95.
14 Runciman to Chamberlain, 21 September 1938. *Correspondence respecting Czechoslovakia September 1938*. Cmd. 5847.
15 Newton to Halifax, 14 September 1938. DBFP 2 No. 800.
16 German wireless announcement, 1 p.m. 15 September 1938. FO 800/304, fo. 292.
17 *Observer*, 24 July 1938.
18 *The Times*, 10 July 1938.
19 *Manchester Guardian*, 10 May 1938.
20 Henderson to Halifax, 20 September 1938. FO 800/309 fo. 325 seq.
21 *Manchester Guardian*, 9 September 1938.
22 *Daily Telegraph*, 9 September 1938.
23 *Sunday Times*, 22 May 1938.
24 Inskip diary, 12 September 1938. INKP 1. Meeting of Ministers, 30 August 1938. CAB 23/94.

25 Beaverbrook–Chamberlain correspondence, 16–17 September 1938. Beaverbrook C/80.
26 Phipps to Halifax, 8 September 1938. DBFP 2 No. 807.
27 Inskip diary, 12 September 1938 (incident of 10 September). INKP 1.
28 Phipps to Halifax, 10 September 1938. DBFP 2 No. 828.
29 Ibid., FO 800/314 fo. 127 seq.
30 Cabinet 38 (38) 14 September. CAB 23/95.
31 Phipps to Halifax, 14 September 1938. DBFP 2 Nos 872, 874.
32 Ibid., 13 September 1938 (copy). PHPP 1/20 fo. 68.
33 Ibid., DBFP 2 No. 857.
34 Ibid., 14 September 1938. FO 800/311 fo. 71 seq.
35 Ibid., (copy). PHPP 1/20 fo. 77.
36 Inskip diary, 13 September 1938. INKP 1.
37 Halifax to Henderson, 5 August 1938 (copy). FO 800/314 fo. 25 seq.
38 Vansittart minute, 29 August 1938. FO 371/22289.
39 Maisky to Lloyd George, 4 October 1938. LG G/14/1/9.
40 Neville to Hilda Chamberlain, 9 October 1937. NC 18/1/1023.
41 Chilston telegram, 14 September 1938. FO 371/21777.
42 Dalton diary, 5 September 1938.
43 Meeting with delegation from National Council of Labour, 17 September 1938 (written 19 September). PREM 1/264 fo. 14 seq.
44 Henderson to Halifax, 1 April 1938. DBFP 1 No. 121.
45 Wilson note, 30 August 1938. PREM 1/266A fo. 263.
46 Neville to Ida Chamberlain, 19 September 1938. NC 18/1/1069.
47 Henderson to Wilson, 9 September 1938. PREM 1/266A fo. 354 seq.
48 Inskip diary, 8 September 1938. INKP 1.
49 Chamberlain to Runciman, 12 September 1938; Newton to Halifax, 13 September 1938. PREM 1/266A fos 320 seq., 319.
50 Neville to Ida Chamberlain, 19 September 1938. NC 18/1/1069.
51 Halifax to Henderson, 13 September 1938. PREM 1/266A fo. 315.
52 Inskip diary, 14 September 1938. INKP 1.
53 Phipps to Halifax, 14 September 1938. DBFP 2 Nos 883, 894.
54 Daily Herald, News Chronicle, Daily Telegraph, 15 September 1938.
55 Chamberlain to Runciman, 12 September 1938 (copy). PREM 1/266A fo. 320 ff.
56 Chamberlain, Notes of conversations . . . DBFP 2 No. 895. Cabinet minutes 39 (38), 17 September. CAB 23/95. Neville to Ida Chamberlain, 19 September 1938. NC 18/1/1069.
57 Cabinet 39 (38) 17 September. CAB 23/95.
58 Inskip diary, 17 September 1938. INKP 1.
59 Vansittart to Halifax, 17 September 1938. FO 800/311 fos 84–5.
60 Record of Anglo-French conversations . . . 18 September 1938. DBFP 2 No. 928. Cabinet 40 (38) 19 September. CAB 23/95.

5 ON THE PRECIPICE

1 Newton to Halifax, 19 September 1938. DBFP 2 No. 959.
2 The Times, 21 September 1938.
3 Daily Herald, 22 September 1938.
4 News Chronicle, 21 September 1938.
5 News Chronicle, 21 September 1938; Daily Herald, 21 September; Daily Telegraph, 20 September.
6 Daily Telegraph, 21 September 1938.
7 Daily Herald, 23 September 1938.
8 The Times, 22 September 1938.
9 Evening Standard, 21 September 1938.

10 Note on whether . . . to fight Germany now or to postpone the issue (Gen. Ismay, 20 September 1938) CAB 21/544.
11 Newton to Halifax, 19 September 1938. DBFP 2 No. 961.
12 Halifax to Newton, 21 September 1938. DBFP No. 991.
13 E. Beneš, *Munich* (Paris: Stock, 1970) pp. 219–27.
14 Cabinet 41 (38), 21 September. CAB 23/95.
15 Vansittart memorandum, 30 August 1938. VNST 2/39.
16 See, e.g., Vansittart to Halifax, 16 September 1938. FO 800/314 fo. 161.
17 Cabinet 41 (38), 21 September. CAB 23/95.
18 For accounts of the meeting, see Cabinet 42 (38), 24 September, CAB 23/95; also DBFP 2 No. 1033.
19 Notes of conversation . . . 22 September 1938. DBFP 2 No. 1033.
20 To High Commissioners, etc., 1.15 a.m. 23 September 1938. CAB 21/587.
21 Cooper to Halifax, Stanley to Halifax, 22 September 1938. FO 800/309 fo. 347 seq., fo. 351.
22 E. L. Spears *et al.* to Halifax, 24 September 1938. FO 800/308 fo. 355.
23 Cabinet 42 (38), 24 September. CAB 23/95.
24 Cabinet 43 (38), 25 September. CAB 23/95.
25 Chamberlain to Halifax, n.d. Hickleton A4.410.3.7.
26 Cabinet 44 (38), 11.30 p.m. 25 September. CAB 23/95.
27 Dalton diary, 25 September 1938.
28 Cabinet 44 (38), 11.30 p.m. 25 September. CAB 23/95.
29 Cabinet 45 (38), 26 September. CAB 23/95.
30 See PREM 1/242 fo. 29 seq.
31 C. T. te Water *aide-mémoire*, 27 September 1938. PREM 1/242 fo. 27.
32 See PREM 1/242 fo. 1 seq.; compare also Tweedsmuir to Chamberlain, 27 October 1938 (ibid., fo. 7) for a statement of reactions after the crisis.
33 See, for example, Halifax's meeting with National Council of Labour, 21 September 1938. PREM 1/264 fo. 2 seq.
34 Cabinet 46 (38), 27 September. CAB 23/95.

6 MUNICH

1 Neville to Hilda Chamberlain, 2 October 1938. NC 18/1/1070.
2 Phipps to Halifax, 26 September 1938. DBFP 2 No. 1106.
3 Newton to Halifax, 27 September 1938. DBFP 2 No. 1148.
4 Ibid., DBFP 2 No. 1130.
5 Ibid., 26 September 1938. DBFP 2 No. 1109
6 Perth to Halifax, 28 September 1938. DBFP 2 No. 1186.
7 Halifax to Henderson, 28 September 1938. DBFP 2 No. 1158.
8 Perth to Halifax, 28 September 1938. DBFP Nos 1166, 1167.
9 *News Chronicle*, 29 September 1938.
10 U.K. Delegation (Munich) to Halifax, 30 September 1938; note by Wilson. DBFP 2 Nos 1224, 1227.
11 Note by Sir H. Wilson, ibid.
12 Cabinet 47 (38), 30 September. CAB 23/95.
13 *Daily Worker*, 1 October 1938.
14 *Daily Herald*, 1 October 1938.
15 *Daily Telegraph*, 30 September 1938.
16 Duff Cooper to Phipps, 20 April 1939. PHPP 3/2 fos 4–5.
17 Tillett to Chamberlain, 26 September 1938. NC 7/11/31/275.
18 Samuel to Chamberlain, 30 September 1938. NC 7/11/31/237.
19 Dalton diary, 3 October 1938.
20 n.d. [3–4 October 1938]. Bodleian MS Eng. Hist. c.597, fo. 101 seq.

21 For analyses of voting see *The Times*, 9 October 1938; *Daily Herald*, 7 October.
22 Maxton to Ponsonby, 16 October 1938. Bodleian MS. Eng. Hist. c.680, fo. 78.
23 Astor memorandum, sent by Hoare to Chamberlain, 14 November 1938. PREM 1/249 fo. 38 seq.
24 Dalton diary, *c.*20 January 1939.
25 Ibid., 8 December 1938, cf. 20 January 1939.
26 See Gilbert Murray's note of Beneš' speech to L.N.U., 12 April 1940. GM 66.
27 Maisky to Lloyd George, 4 October 1938. L.G. G/14/1/9; Dalton diary, 11 October.

7 AFTERMATH

1 Neville to Ida Chamberlain, 22 October 1938. NC 18/1/1074.
2 Chamberlain to Runciman, 20 October 1938. WR 289.
3 Runciman to Halifax, 25 October 1938 (copy). WR 289.
4 Neville to Ida Chamberlain, 22 October 1938. NC 18/1/1074.
5 Ibid.
6 Ms. note, 26 October 1938. Samuel A/111 fos 1–5.
7 Samuel–Crewe correspondence, 25–27 October 1938. Samuel A/111 fos 4–8; Crewe C/44.
8 Henderson to Halifax, 20 September 1938. FO 800/269 fo. 294.
9 *The Times*, 26 September 1938.
10 Amery to Beaverbrook, 7 October 1938. Beaverbrook C/7.
11 Cadogan to Halifax, 15 October 1938. FO 371/21659 fo. 43 seq.
12 Hankey to Phipps, 11 November 1938. PHPP 3/3 fo. 93 seq.
13 Cabinet 53 (38), 7 November. CAB 23/96.
14 Relative air strengths . . . 25 October 1938. CP 218 (38). CAB 24/279.
15 Note on the question of whether . . . to fight Germany now . . . 20 September 1938. CAB 21/544.
16 Cabinet 53 (38), 7 November. CAB 23/96.
17 Ashton-Gwatkin notes, 27 October 1938. FO 371/21659 fo. 53 seq.
18 Cadogan to Halifax, 15 October 1938, and notes. FO 371/21659 fo. 43 seq.
19 Halifax to Phipps, 1 November 1938. PHPP 1/21 fos 58–62.
20 Astor memorandum, enclosed in Hoare to Chamberlain, 14 November 1938. PREM 1/249 fo. 36 seq.
21 Henderson to Halifax, 12, 13, 14 October 1938. FO 371/21658 fos 241 seq., 244 seq., 247 seq.
22 Ogilvie-Forbes to Halifax, 24 October 1938. FO 371/21658 fo. 270 seq.
23 Phipps to Halifax, 24 October 1938 (copy). PHPP 1/21 fo. 4.
24 Dominions Office meeting, 1 December 1938. FO 371/21593 fo. 7 seq.
25 Neville to Ida Chamberlain, 13 November 1938. NC 18/1/1076.
26 FP (36) 32nd Meeting, 14 November 1938. CAB 27/624.
27 Phipps to Halifax, 4 November 1938. FO 800/311 fo. 143 seq.
28 Ibid., 1 October 1938. DBFP 3 No. 100.
29 Hankey to Phipps, 1–3 October 1938 (copy). HNKY 5/5 fo. 79.
30 Halifax to Phipps, 28 October 1938. PHPP 1/21 fo. 21.
31 F.O. memorandum, 16 November 1938. FO 371/21592 fo. 290 seq.
32 W. Strang memorandum, 17 November 1938. FO 371/21592 fo. 266 seq.
33 Visit of British Ministers to Paris, 24 November 1938. CP 269 (38), 26 November. FO 371/21592 fo. 353 seq.
34 Neville to Hilda Chamberlain, 11 December 1938. NC 18/1/1079.
35 Chamberlain to Phipps, 8 December 1938. PHPP 3/1 fo. 60.
36 Perth to Halifax, 16 November 1938 (copy). FO 371/22416 fo. 64 seq.
37 Cabinet 58 (38), 7 December. CAB 23/96. Halifax–Perth correspondence, 1 December 1938. DBFP 3 Nos 462, 464.

38 Neville to Ida Chamberlain, 4 December 1938. NC 18/1/1078.
39 Neville to Hilda Chamberlain, 11 December 1938. NC 18/1/1079.
40 Cadogan to Perth, 12 December 1938; Perth to Halifax, 15 December. DBFP 3 Nos 475, 477.
41 Neville to Ida Chamberlain, 8 January 1939. NC 18/1/1081.
42 Inskip diary, 16 January 1939. INKP 1.
43 Neville to Hilda Chamberlain, 15 January 1939. NC 18/1/1082.
44 Notes of conversations with Mussolini, January 1939. PREM 1/327.
45 Dominions Office meeting, 1 December 1938. FO 371/21593 fo. 7 seq.

8 POPULAR FRONT

 1 Dalton diary, 21 September 1938.
 2 Sinclair to Crewe, 22 June 1938. Crewe C/30.
 3 Neville to Hilda Chamberlain, 27 February 1938. NC 18/1/1040.
 4 Lloyd George to Mottistone, 9 October 1938. L.G. G/13/4/4.
 5 Hirst to Samuel, 5 October 1938. Samuel A/110 fo. 33.
 6 Lothian to Henderson, 13 September 1937. FO 800/268 fo. 267.
 7 Martin Gilbert, *Winston S. Churchill* Vol. v (London, 1976) p. 874 seq.
 8 Churchill's sources of information. Hankey note, incomplete, dated 1938. HNKY 5/1 fo. 125.
 9 LPEC vol. 76, pp. 376–87: NEC meeting, 27 April 1938.
10 LP NEC, 12 April, 25 May 1938. LPEC vol. 76, pp. 271, 434.
11 See, e.g., Crewe to Sinclair, 28 February 1938, THRS 2/38/7; Sinclair to Lothian (copy), 28 February 1938, THRS 2/38/24; Spender to Harris, 5 April 1938, THRS 3/38/1.
12 Sinclair to Harcourt Johnstone ('Crinks'), 1 March 1938 (copy). THRS 3/38/2.
13 See *Liberal Magazine*, 1938, pp. 244–6.
14 Acland to Sinclair, 27 June 1938. THRS 2/38/1.
15 Dalton diary, 3 October 1938.
16 Ibid., 6 October 1938.
17 Churchill to Lloyd George, 17 October, 10 December 1938. L.G. G/4/5/33, 34.
18 Halifax to Chamberlain, 11 October 1938. NC 7/11/31/1244.
19 Dalton diary, 12 October 1938.
20 See LPEC vol. 78, p. 851 seq.
21 Ibid., p. 855 seq.
22 Sinclair to Countess of Aberdeen, 12 December 1938 (copy). THRS 2/38/1.
23 See THRS 3/39/14.
24 Dalton II 3/1, fo. 24 seq.
25 *Daily Herald*, 24 February 1939.
26 Harold Glanville to Harcourt Johnstone, 14 March 1939 (copy). THRS 3/39/8.
27 Sinclair to Raymond Jones, 16 March 1939 (copy). THRS 3/39/8.
28 Neville to Ida Chamberlain, 9 April 1939. NC 18/1/1093.

9 DANGER SIGNALS

 1 Col. W. Fraser to Phipps, 29 December 1938. DBFP 3 No. 509.
 2 Possible German intentions . . . FP (36) 74. FO 371/22961 fo. 244 seq.
 3 Cabinet 5 (39), 2 February. CAB 23/97.
 4 Cadogan memorandum, 26 February 1939. FO 800/294 fo. 28 seq.
 5 Halifax to Mallet, 24 January 1939. DBFP 4 No. 5.
 6 See, e.g., Vereker to Halifax, 28 December 1938; Mason – Macfarlane memorandum, 26 December; Vereker to Halifax, 10 January 1939. DBFP 3 Nos 503 505, 529.
 7 Possible German aggression against Holland . . . 27 January 1939. CP 3 (39), CAB

24/282. For Dutch view see Cabinet 7 (39), 15 February. CAB 23/97.

8 Henderson to Halifax, 18 February 1939. DBFP 4 No. 1

9 Cabinet 3 (39), 1 February. CAB 23/97.

10 Halifax to Mallet, 24 January 1939. DBFP 4 No. 5.

11 Cabinet 3 (39), 1 February. CAB 23/97.

12 Phipps to Eden, 6 October 1937 (copy). PHPP 1/19 fo. 14.

13 Enclosure from Inskip in Sargent to Phipps, 29 November 1938 (copy). FO 371/21675.

14 Cabinet 1 (39), 18 January. CAB 23/97.

15 Phipps to Halifax, 10 February 1939 (copy). PHPP 1/22 fo. 14.

16 Cabinet 6 (39), 8 February. CAB 23/97.

17 Phipps to Halifax, 5 February 1939 (copy). PHPP 1/22 fo. 6.

18 Neville to Ida Chamberlain, 26 February 1939. NC 18/1/1087.

19 Vansittart memorandum for Halifax, 19 December 1938. FO 371/22922 fo. 19 seq.

20 Strang to Ismay 12, January 1939 (copy), quoting Col. Fraser's analysis in Phipps despatch, 28 December 1938. CAB 53/43 pp. 176–7.

21 Manuscript comment, 23 January 1939, on Vansittart memorandum. FO 371/22922 fos 37–8.

22 Vansittart, Cadogan to Halifax, 24 January 1939. FO 371/22922, fo. 39.

23 Phipps to Halifax, 29 January 1939. DBFP 4 No. 52.

24 State of preparedness . . . C.I.G.S. memorandum, 19 December 1938. CAB 53/43 fo. 35 seq.

25 Ibid.

26 Cabinet 5 (39), 2 February. CAB 23/97.

27 Cabinet 8 (39), 22 February. CAB 23/97.

28 Halifax to Phipps, 3 February 1939. DBFP 4 No. 81.

29 Ibid., 22 February 1939 (copy). FO 371/22922 fo. 132.

30 Phipps to Halifax, 11, 15 March 1939. FO 371/22922, fos 350, 354.

31 Ogilvie-Forbes to Strang, 25 January 1939. FO 371/22988 fo. 65 seq.

32 Neville to Hilda Chamberlain, 5 February 1939. NC 18/1/1084.

33 Neville to Ida Chamberlain, 12 February 1938. NC 18/1/1085.

34 Henderson to Halifax, 16 February 1939. FO 371/22988 fo. 166 seq.

35 Draft telegram to Canada, Australia, New Zealand, South Africa and Eire Governments, 7 March 1939. CAB 21/540.

36 Cabinet 10 (39), 8 March. CAB 23/97.

10 THE END OF CZECHOSLOVAKIA

1 British Guarantee to Czechoslovakia: memorandum by SSFA, 12 November 1938. CP 258 (38). CAB 24/280 fo. 13 seq.

2 Neville to Hilda Chamberlain, 27 November 1938. NC 18/1/1077.

3 Cabinet 57 (38), 30 November. CAB 23/96.

4 Newton to Halifax, 11 December 1938. DBFP 3 No. 423.

5 F.O. memorandum (unsigned), 9 January 1939. FO 371/22991 fo. 247 seq.

6 Phipps to Halifax, 9 January 1939. FO 371/22991 fo. 20.

7 The visit to Rome . . . CP 8 (39). CAB 24/282 fo. 79 seq.

8 Ibid.

9 Ogilvie-Forbes to Halifax, 8 February 1939; Henderson to Halifax 3 March. DBFP 4 Nos 91, 171.

10 Newton to Halifax, 8 March 1939. FO 371/22991 fo. 124.

11 Cabinet 56 (38), 22 November. CAB 23/96.

12 DBFP 3 Nos 83, 85, 86, 91, 97.

13 See tables from *Central European Observer*, 16 December 1938. FO 371/22893 fo. 11.

14 Newton to Strang, 22 October 1938. FO 371/21579 fo. 122 seq.

15 F.O. minute by R. L. Speaight, 28 January 1939. FO 371/22893 fo. 38 seq:

16 Newton to Halifax, 20 December 1938. FO 371/21580 fo. 298.
17 Troutbeck to Halifax, 26 January 1939. FO 371/22896 fo. 53.
18 Newton to Halifax, 17 January 1939. FO 371/22896 fo. 33.
19 R. L. Speaight minute, after conversation with Major McNeill Moss, 28 January 1939. FO 371/22893 fo. 38 seq.
20 Ogilvie-Forbes to Halifax, 24 January 1939. DBFP 4 No. 4.
21 Ibid., 23 January 1939. DBFP 4 No. 2.
22 Newton to Halifax, 6 March 1939. DBFP 4 No. 185.
23 Departmental note by Speaight, 10 March 1939. FO 371/22896 fo. 180.
24 Henderson to Halifax, 10 March 1939. DBFP 4 No. 197.
25 Newton to Halifax, 11 March 1938. FO 371/22896 fo. 214.
26 Ibid., 21 March 1939. FO 371/22897 fo. 212 seq.
27 Kennard to Halifax, 7 March 1939. FO 371/22896 fo. 190.
28 See Daily Telegraph, 20, 24 March 1939.
29 Halifax to Henderson (copy), 15 March 1939. CAB 21/588.
30 Newton to Halifax, 31 March 1939 (printed copy). CAB 21/589.
31 Newton to Halifax, 15 March 1939. FO 371/22897 fo. 64. Knox (Budapest) to Halifax, 14 March. FO 371/23108 fo. 96.
32 Vološin to Halifax (telegram), 15 March 1939. FO 371/22897 fo. 41.
33 Knox to Halifax, 17 March 1939. FO 371/23108 fo. 136.
34 Ibid., 20 March 1939. FO 371/23108 fo. 177.

11 PREPARING FOR THE INEVITABLE

1 Cabinet 11 (39), 15 March. CAB 23/98.
2 F. N. Mason-Macfarlane to Henderson, 18 March 1939. CAB 21/588.
3 Daily Express, 17 March 1939.
4 Daily Telegraph, 15 March 1939.
5 The Times, 16 March 1939.
6 Daily Express, 15 March 1939.
7 Daily Mail, 15 March 1939.
8 The Times, 21 March 1976.
9 T. F. Tweed to Lloyd George, 16 March 1939. L.G. G/28/2/12.
10 See account in PREM 1/322.
11 Dalton diary, 23 March 1939.
12 Ibid.
13 Cabinet 12 (39), 18 March. CAB 23/98.
14 Cabinet 13 (39), 20 March. CAB 23/98.
15 Daily Express, 22 March 1939.
16 Ibid., 23 March 1939.
17 Phipps to Halifax, 15 March 1939. DBFP 4 Nos 279, 276.
18 Record of conversations . . . 21–22 March 1939. CP 73 (39). CAB 24/284.
19 Neville to Ida Chamberlain, 26 March 1939. NC 18/1/1091.
20 Ibid.
21 Sir R. Hoare (Bucharest) to Halifax, 21 March 1939. FO 371/23108 fo. 189.
22 FP (36) 38th meeting, 27 March 1939. CAB 24/284.
23 Neville to Hilda Chamberlain, 2 April 1939. NC 1/18/1092.
24 Privy Council Report to Runciman, 3 April 1939. WR 298.
25 Runciman to Chamberlain, 31 March 1939 (2). NC 7/11/32/225.
26 Hankey to Phipps, 4 April 1939. PHPP 3/3 fo. 99 seq.
27 Neville to Ida Chamberlain, 26 March 1939. NC 18/1/1091.
28 Ibid., 9 April 1939. NC 1/18/1093.
29 Ibid.
30 Runciman to Chamberlain, 31 March 1939 (1). NC 7/11/32/224.

31 Wilson to Chamberlain, 21 October 1938. PREM 1/336.
32 See various documents, January-February 1939, in CAB 24/283.
33 Wilson to Chamberlain, 9 April 1939; Chatfield to Chamberlain, 10 April. PRE 1/336.
34 Inskip note for Cabinet, 2 February 1939. CAB 24/283.
35 Privy Council report to Runciman, 3 April 1939. WR 298.
36 Cabinet 15 (39), 29 March. CAB 23/98.
37 Ibid.
38 Cabinet meeting, 10 February 1939. U.R.O. CAB 4/410.
39 Cabinet meeting, 25 July 1939. U.R.O. CAB 4/422.
40 Ogilvie-Forbes to Cadogan, 10 April 1939. FO 800/294 fo. 37.
41 Seeds to Oliphant, 21 February 1939. FO 371/23697 fo. 65.

Bibliography

As the author has explained, the present book is an attempt to understand the story of the Year of Munich in the light of documents from the period itself – mainly primary materials which have only become available for inspection in the last few years; and he has deliberately tried to exclude from his mind most of the comment from intervening years which was written before these primary documents became available. For that reason there is not much reference in the text to secondary sources, and it appears rather inappropriate to compile an extensive bibliography of such material. For those are interested in following up the documents, very useful bibliographies will be found in such works as Maurice Cowling's recent book, *The Impact of Hitler*, and in older sources such as A. J. P. Taylor's *English History 1914–1945* and his *Origins of the Second World War*.

The sources here used are – inevitably – incomplete, and more documents are constantly becoming available; but the author feels that we have now reached a point where at least an interim 'over-all view' may be taken. Nevertheless, the reader will detect some imbalance. The author has not been able, for example, to see the papers of Winston Churchill or Sir John Simon. The papers of Neville Chamberlain, which became available for scholarly study in the middle of 1975, seem to give a good insight into the Prime Minister's mind; but the available papers from other senior members of his Government are in some cases perfunctory. On the Labour side, there are also difficulties. The Labour Party Executive Committee minutes and other documents are available (would this were so of all political parties) and Hugh Dalton's diaries are highly revealing; but unfortunately the Clement Attlee papers for the period are scanty and the papers of most Labour Members have not been seen. On the Liberal side we are more fortunate, in that there is a good deal of fascinating material from several of the Party's leading statesmen. With all parties, however – and particularly with Labour – the reader must be warned against the danger of subconsciously attributing to those statesmen whose documents have survived a greater importance, and to those whose documents have been lost or are unavailable lesser importance, than they truly possess. With the documents consulted at the Public Record Office (and particularly with the diplomatic correspondence of the FO 371 series) the problem is somewhat different; for the bulk of material is so vast that it is virtually impossible to work through it all, and there doubtless remain undiscovered many valuable nuggets.

The principal archive sources used are as follows:

Vyvyan Adams papers, London School of Economics

A. V. Alexander (Earl Alexander of Hillsborough) papers, Churchill College, Cambridge

Clement Attlee (Earl Attlee) papers, University College, Oxford

Lord Beaverbrook papers, Beaverbrook Library (now at House of Lords Records Office)

Cabinet papers, Public Record Office, London (P.R.O.):
    Cabinet Office papers (CAB 21)
    Cabinet Minutes (CAB 23)
    Cabinet Memoranda (CAB 24)
    Cabinet Committee on Foreign Policy Minutes (CAB 27)
    Committee of Imperial Defence: Chiefs of Staff Sub-Committee (CAB 53)

Sir Alexander Cadogan papers, FO 800 series, P.R.O.

Neville Chamberlain papers, PREM files, P.R.O.

Neville Chamberlain papers, University of Birmingham

Lord Chatfield papers, National Maritime Museum, Greenwich

Viscount Cranborne (6th Marquess of Salisbury) papers, FO 800 series, P.R.O.

Marquess of Crewe papers, University Library, Cambridge

Harry Crookshank (Viscount Crookshank) papers, Bodleian Library, Oxford

Hugh Dalton (Lord Dalton) papers, London School of Economics

Foreign Office papers, P.R.O. Diplomatic correspondence (FO 371) and individual archives (FO 800)

David Lloyd George (Earl Lloyd-George of Dwyfor) papers, Beaverbrook Library, London (now at House of Lords)

Viscount Halifax (Earl Halifax) papers, FO 800 series, P.R.O.

Viscount Halifax papers (Hickleton papers: microfilm), Churchill College, Cambridge

Sir Nevile Henderson papers, FO 800 series, P.R.O.

Sir Samuel Hoare (Viscount Templewood) papers, University Library, Cambridge

Sir Thomas Inskip (1st Viscount Caldecote) papers, Churchill College, Cambridge

Labour Party Executive Committe minutes, etc., Labour Party, Transport House, London

Labour Spain Committee papers, Churchill College, Cambridge

David Margesson (Lord Margesson) papers, Churchill College, Cambridge

Gilbert Murray papers, Bodleian Library, Oxford

Sir Eric Phipps papers, Churchill College, Cambridge

Lord Ponsonby papers, Bodleian Library, Oxford

Viscount Runciman papers, FO 800 series, P.R.O.

Viscount Runciman papers, University of Newcastle upon Tyne
Viscount Samuel papers, House of Lords Record Office
Sir Archibald Sinclair (Viscount Thurso) papers, Churchill College, Cambridge
Ulster Record Office papers: Minutes of Northern Ireland Cabinet, Ulster Record Office, Belfast
Sir Robert Vansittart (Lord Vansittart) papers, Churchill College, Cambridge.
Reference has also been made to the following newspapers and periodicals:

Annual Register
Birmingham Post
Daily Express
Daily Herald
Daily Herald
Daily Mail
Daily Mirror
Daily Sketch
Daily Telegraph
Daily Worker
Evening Standard

Glasgow Herald
Hansard (H.C. Deb. 5.s.)
Manchester Guardian
News Chronicle
Observer
Star
Sunday Times
Le Temps
The Times
Yorkshire Post

Index

Index